BEANO®

WHERE'S GNASHER?

think you can find me? You've got gno chance!

First published in Great Britain 2019
This edition published in Great Britain 2023 by Farshore
An imprint of HarperCollins*Publishers*, 1 London Bridge Street, London, SE1 9GF
www.farshore.co.uk

HarperCollins*Publishers*
Macken House, 39/40 Mayor Street Upper, Dublin 1, D01 C9W8, Ireland

Illustrated by Laura Howell

BEANO.COM

A Beano Studios Product © DC Thomson Ltd (2023)

ISBN 978 0 0085 3421 9
Printed in Italy
001

Stay safe online. Any website addresses listed in this book are correct at the time of going to print.
However, Farshore is not responsible for content hosted by third parties. Please be aware that
online content can be subject to change and websites can contain content that is unsuitable for
children. We advise that all children are supervised when using the internet.

FSC
www.fsc.org

MIX
Paper | Supporting
responsible forestry
FSC™ C007454

This book is produced from independently certified FSC™ paper
to ensure responsible forest management.

For more information visit: www.harpercollins.co.uk/green

GNASHER IS MISSING!

Beanotown is home to many weird and wonderful inhabitants: from the yeti that works in the school library and the headless headmaster of Horrible Hall to the ghostly librarian and the mysterious tribe of Vikings who founded Beanotown 1,000 years ago. However, there are none more wonderful than Gnasher, his owner Dennis and their friends and family.

Can you track them down as they travel across Beanotown in search of Gnasher?

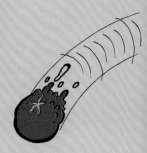

Gnasher

The Abyssinian wire–haired tripe hound is Dennis's best friend and partner in crime, and he's gone missing! Gnasher's favourite thing in the world is Dennis, and he would do anything for him (and a delicious sausage).

Dennis Menace

Dennis is always in trouble – and it's not always his fault. If trouble comes knocking, it comes knocking for Dennis. When his best friend Gnasher goes missing, Dennis leads a search party through Beanotown.

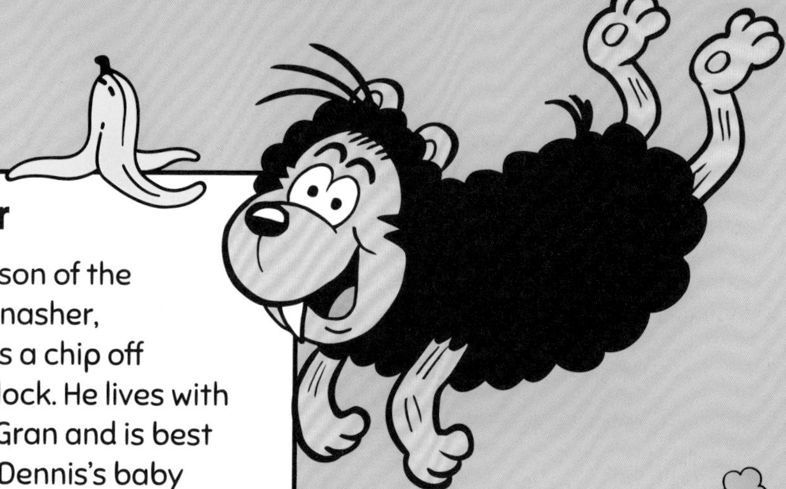

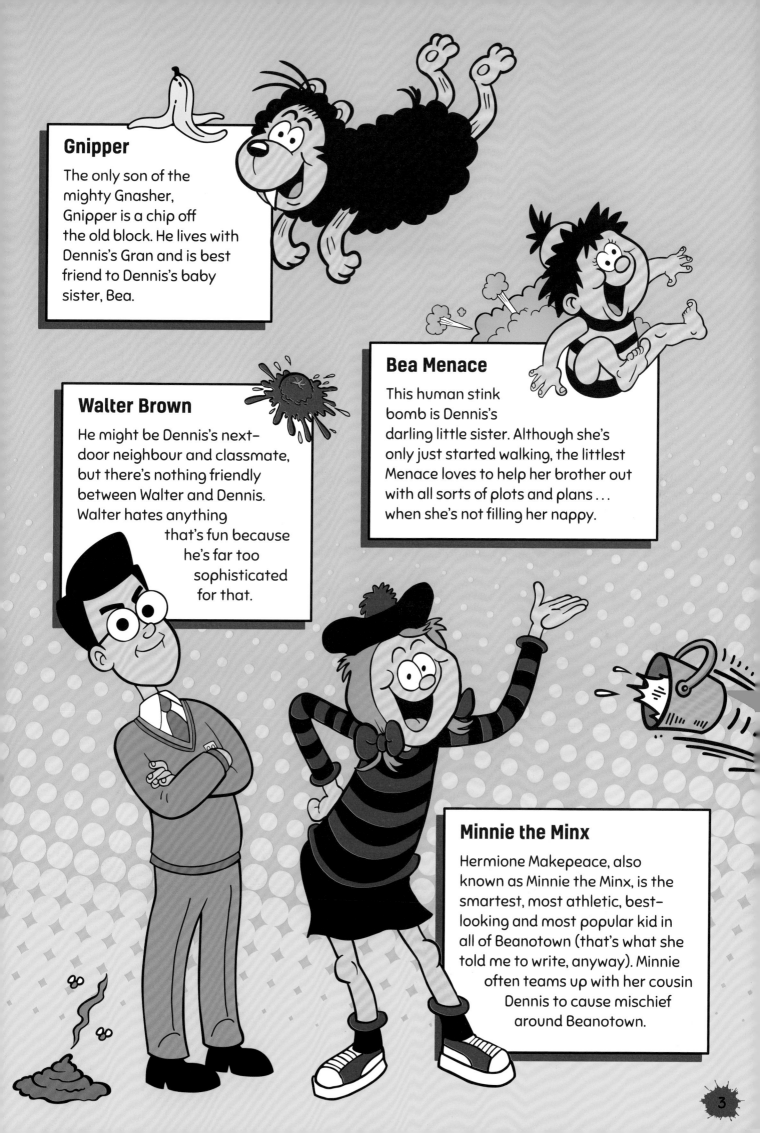

Gnipper

The only son of the mighty Gnasher, Gnipper is a chip off the old block. He lives with Dennis's Gran and is best friend to Dennis's baby sister, Bea.

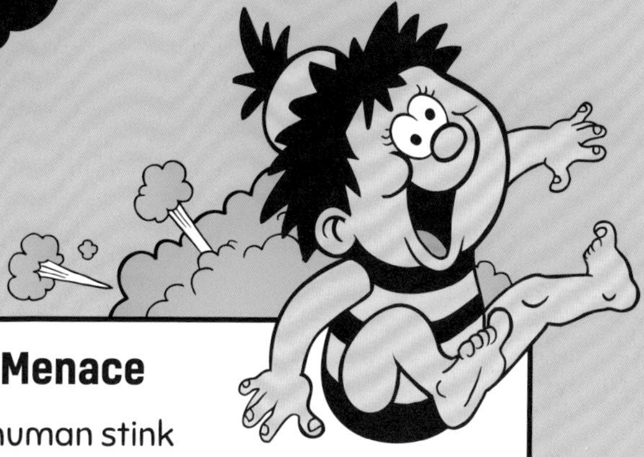

Bea Menace

This human stink bomb is Dennis's darling little sister. Although she's only just started walking, the littlest Menace loves to help her brother out with all sorts of plots and plans . . . when she's not filling her nappy.

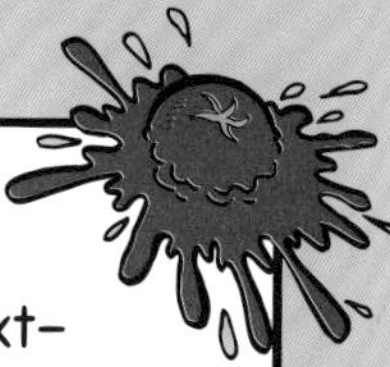

Walter Brown

He might be Dennis's next-door neighbour and classmate, but there's nothing friendly between Walter and Dennis. Walter hates anything that's fun because he's far too sophisticated for that.

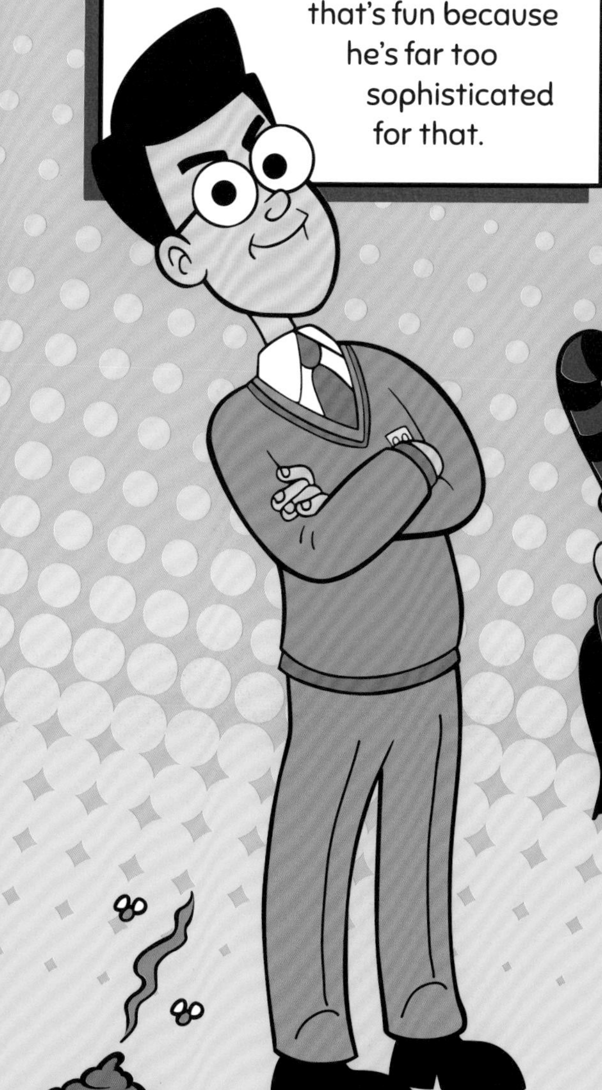

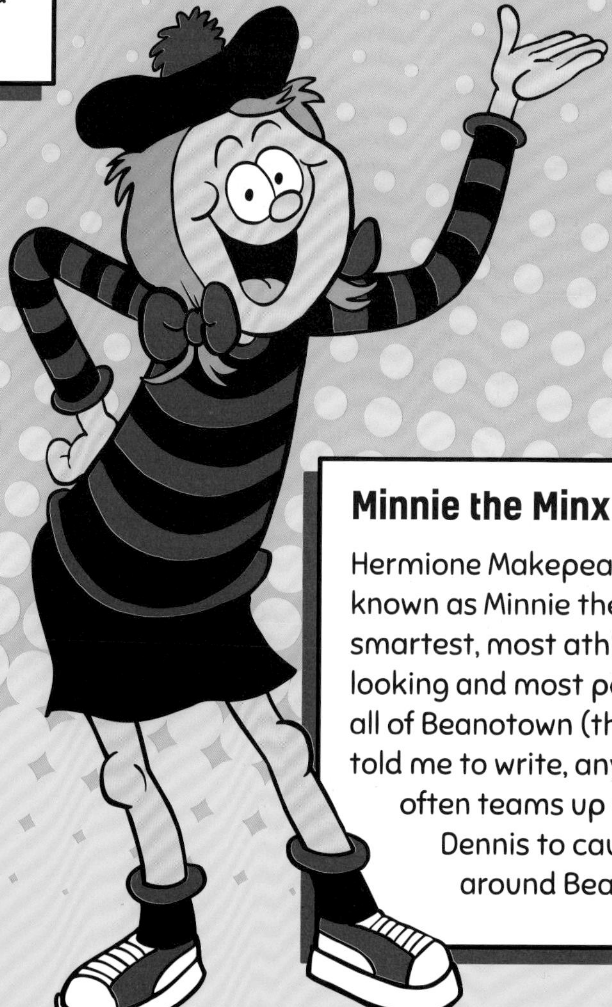

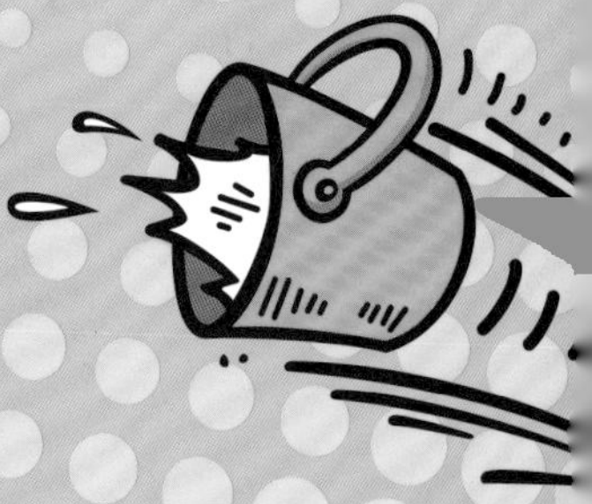

Minnie the Minx

Hermione Makepeace, also known as Minnie the Minx, is the smartest, most athletic, best-looking and most popular kid in all of Beanotown (that's what she told me to write, anyway). Minnie often teams up with her cousin Dennis to cause mischief around Beanotown.

LOCATIONS

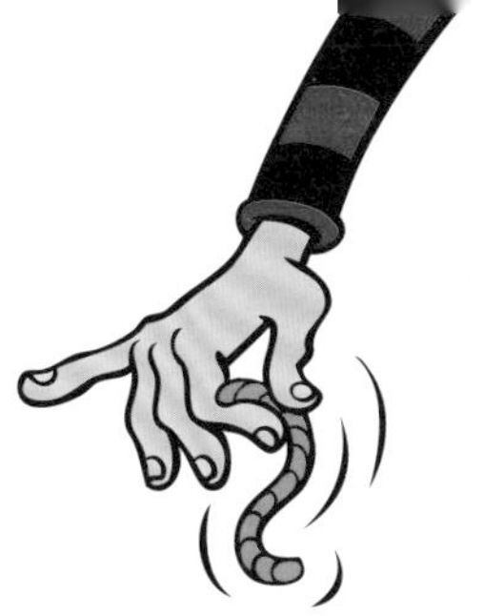

Welcome to this pleasant, quiet town where citizens walk the streets free from the fear of pranks, monsters or chaos. Oh, wait! I'm mistaken. This is Beanotown – where chaos rules supreme and a boy named Dennis has lost his canine companion.

Search the pages to see if you can find the Abyssinian wire-haired tripe hound, affectionally known as Gnasher, as well as Dennis, Minnie, Gnipper, Walter and Bea as they go on a dog hunt across town. At the back of the book, there's also a super-long list of other Beano characters and objects to search for. I dare you to find them all!

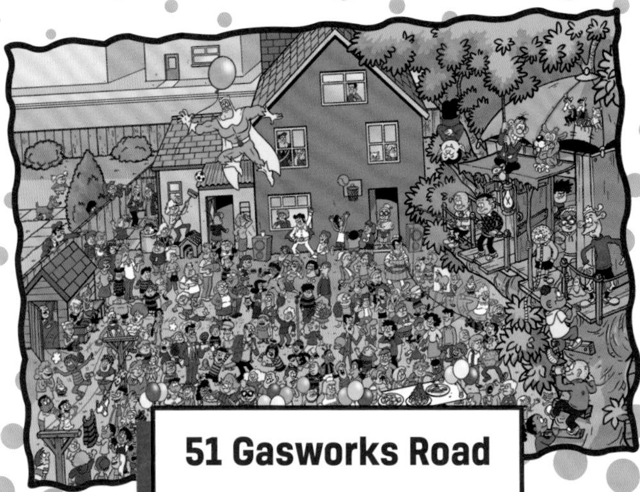

51 Gasworks Road

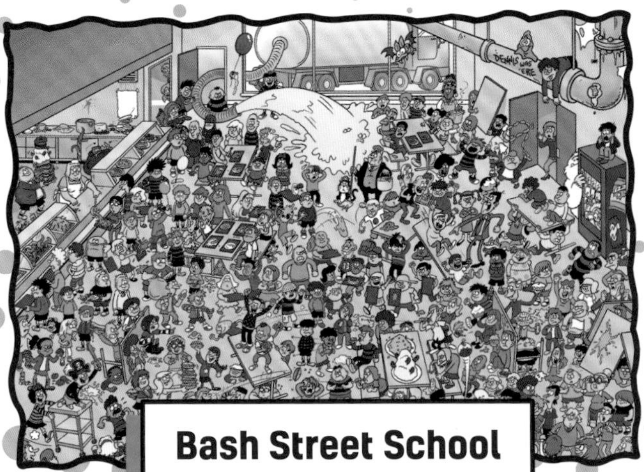

Bash Street School

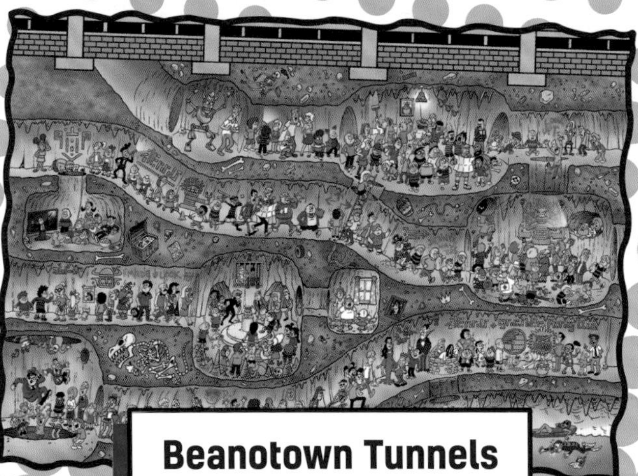

Beanotown Tunnels

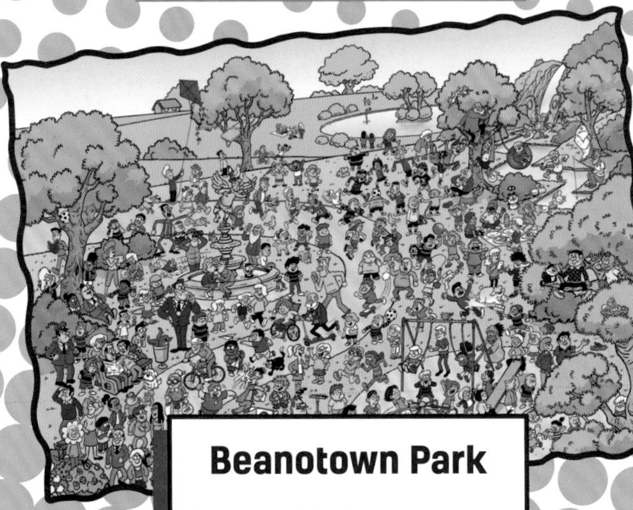

Beanotown Park

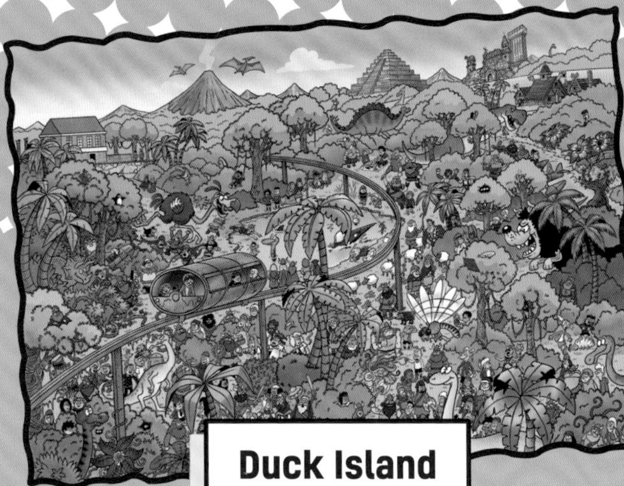

Duck Island

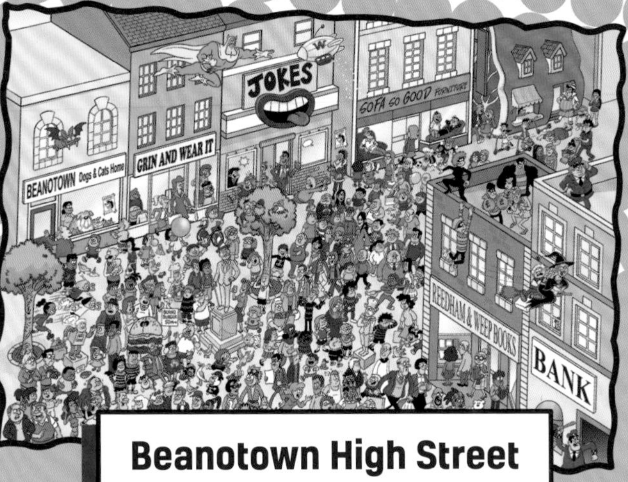
JOKES
GRIN AND WEAR IT
BANK

Beanotown High Street

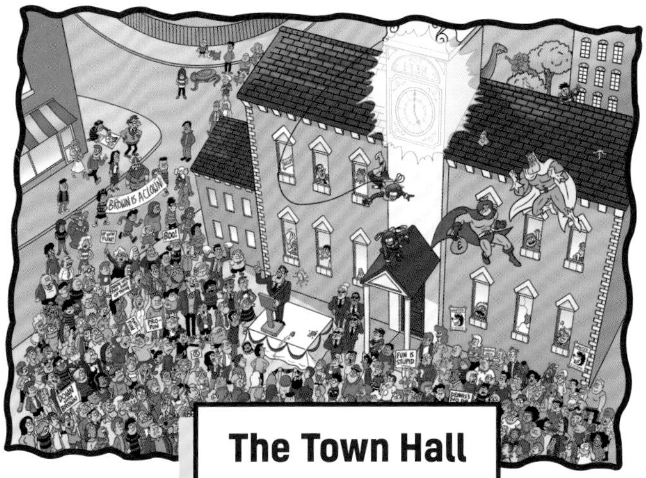

The Town Hall

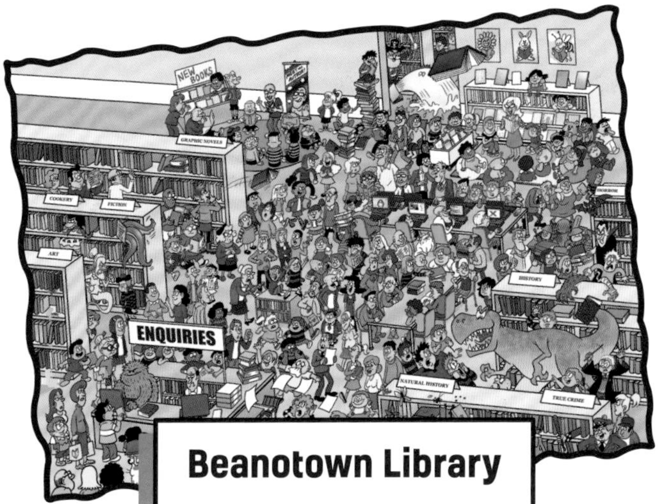
NEW BOOKS
ENQUIRIES

Beanotown Library

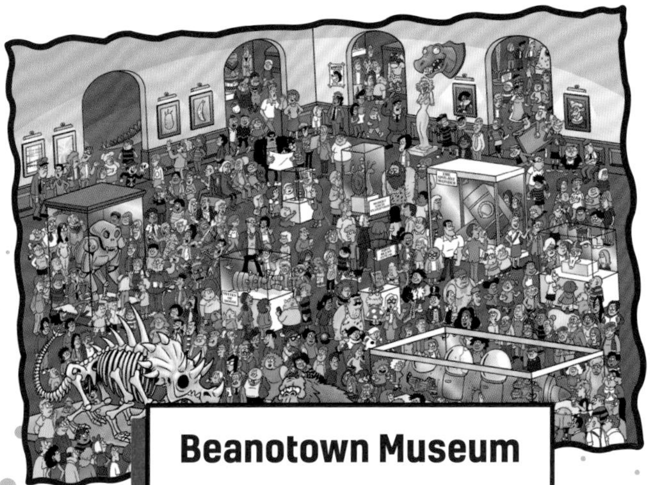

Beanotown Museum

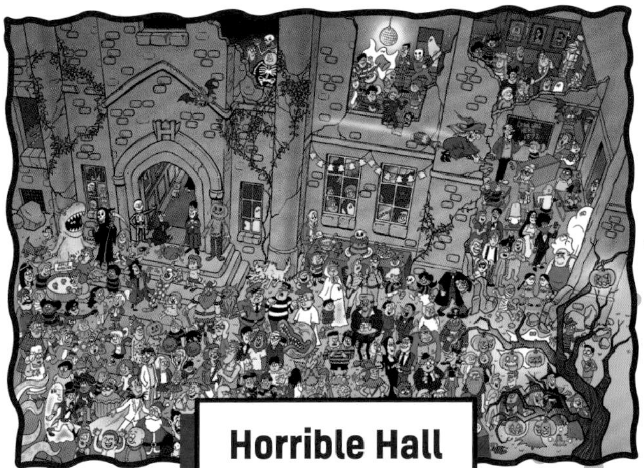

Horrible Hall

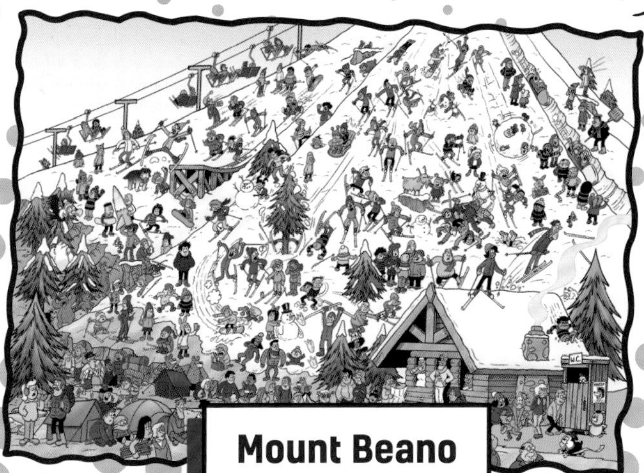

Mount Beano

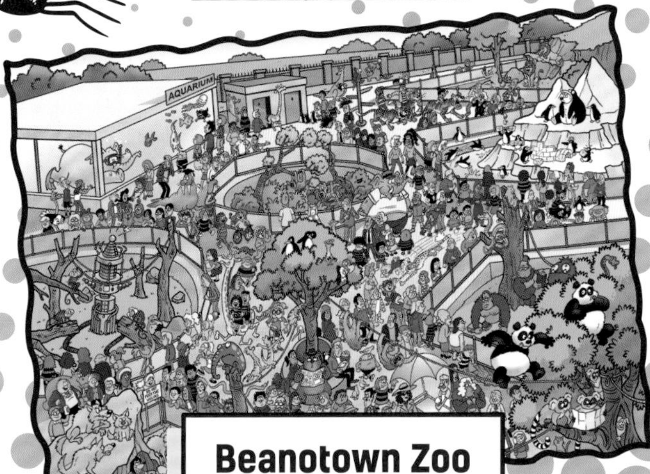
AQUARIUM

Beanotown Zoo

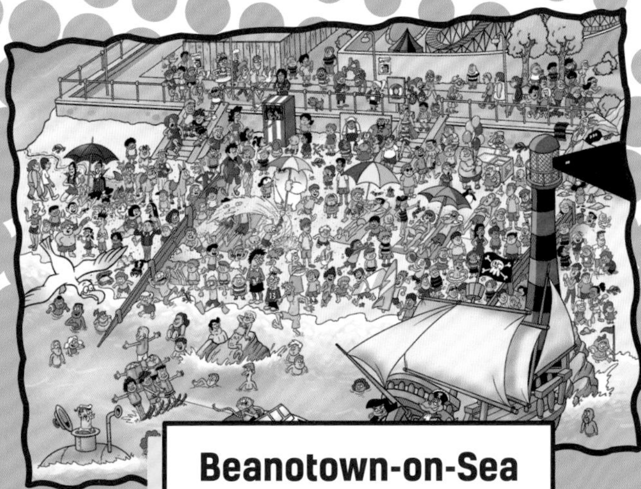

Beanotown-on-Sea

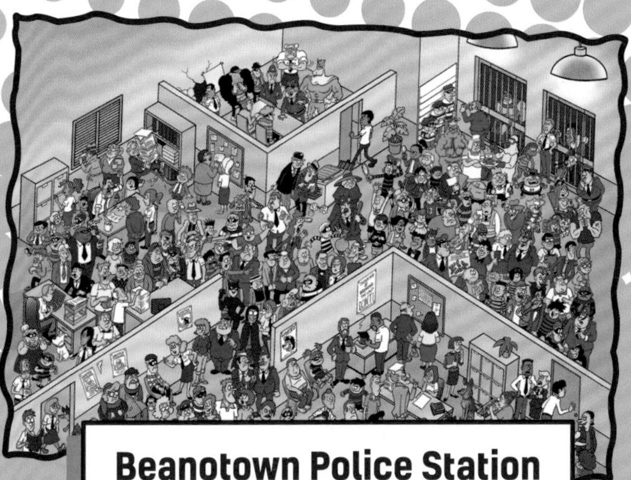

Beanotown Police Station

51 Gasworks Road

This is the home of the Menace family, and today it's Dennis Senior's birthday. He didn't want to have a party, but Gran made a cake and it seems as though the entire town has turned up for a slice! In the free-for-all cake scrum, Dennis has lost sight of Gnasher. Can you spot this unspotted dog?

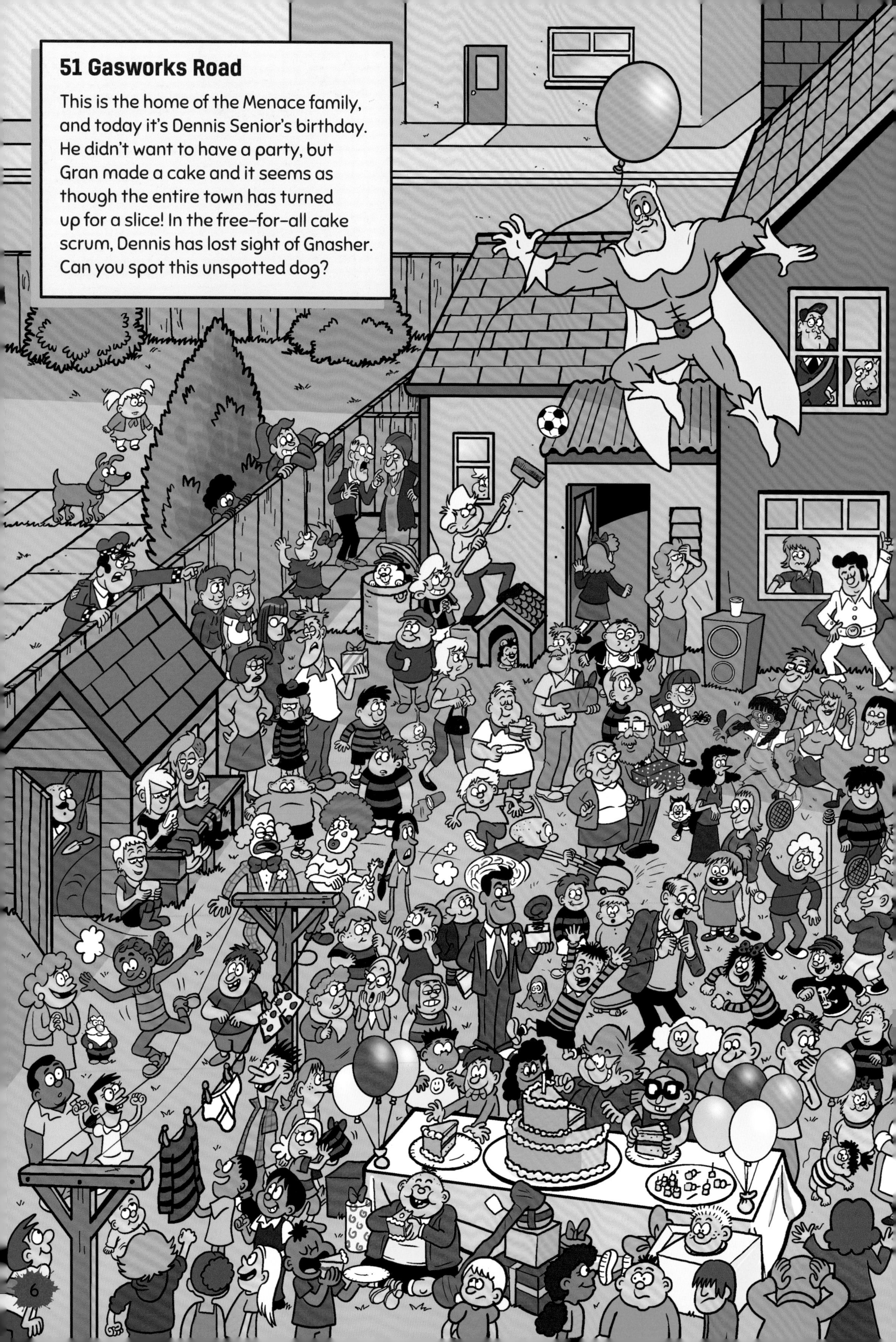

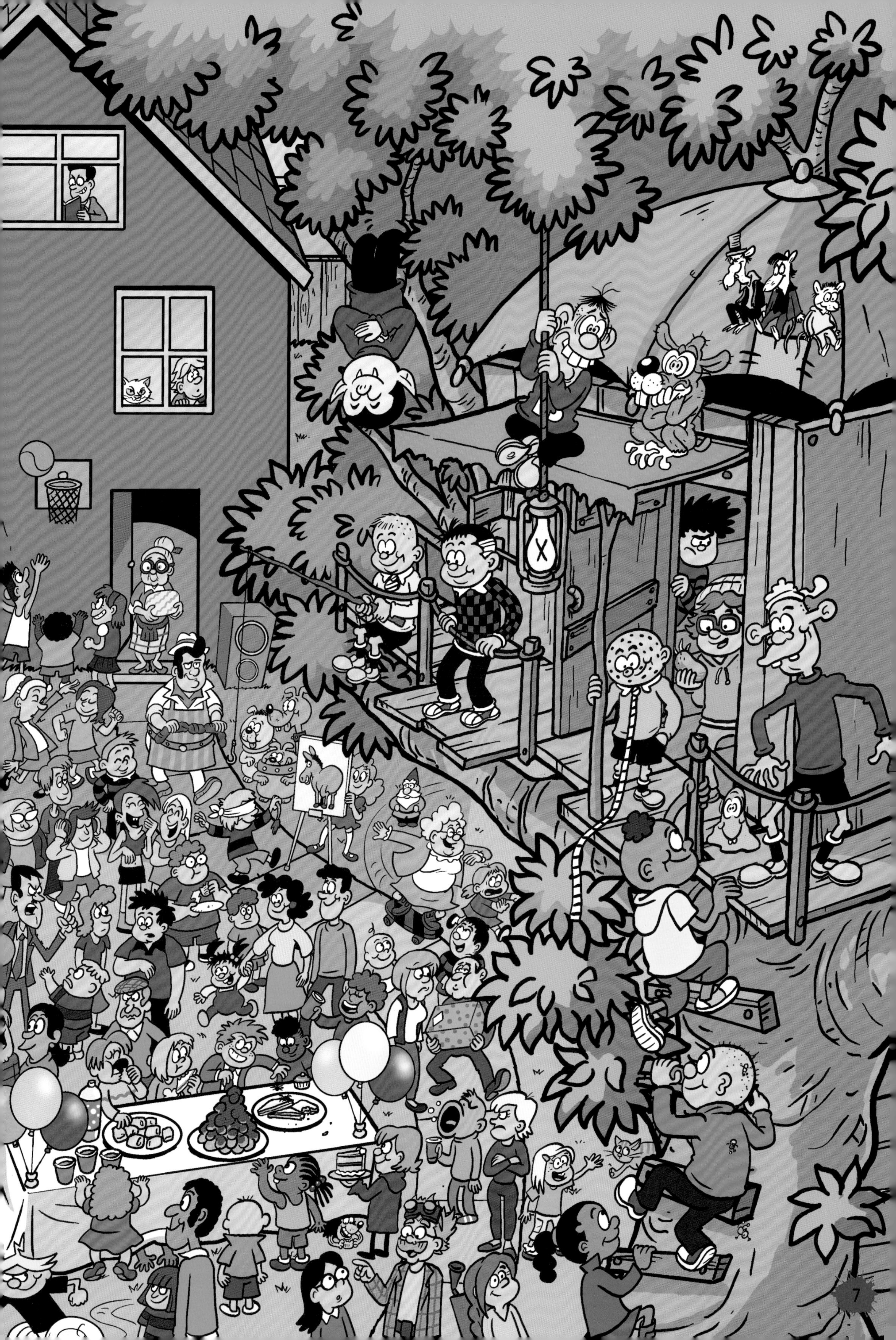

Bash Street School

This is a place of learning, discipline and respect. That is, until it's lunchtime, when it starts to resemble a chimp enclosure. The Bash Street Kids have decided to start a food fight – why? No one cares. You'd better watch out, though, as Olive and Olive make rock cakes that are . . . well . . . like rocks. Can you see Gnasher among the flying food?

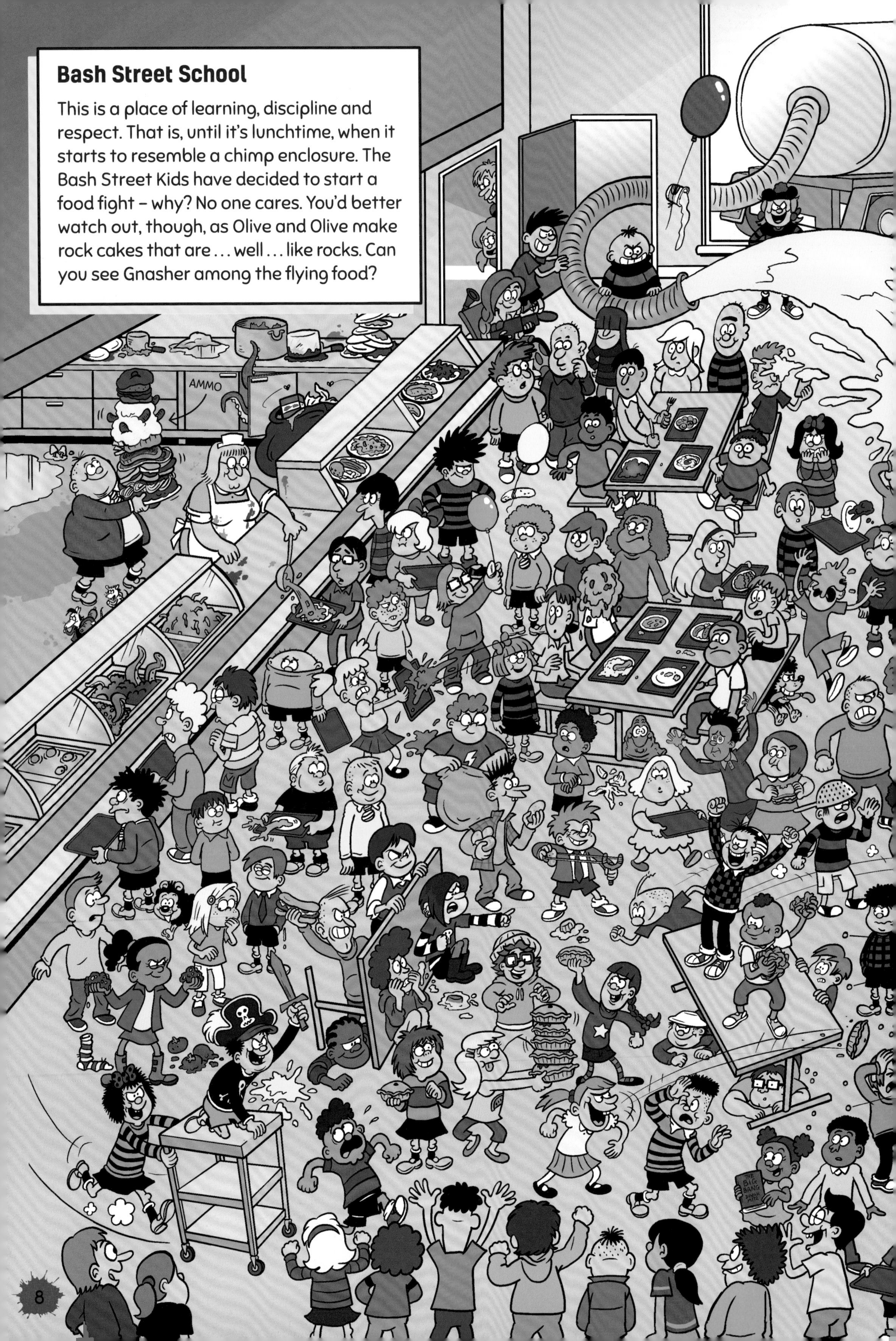
AMMO
THE BIG BANG

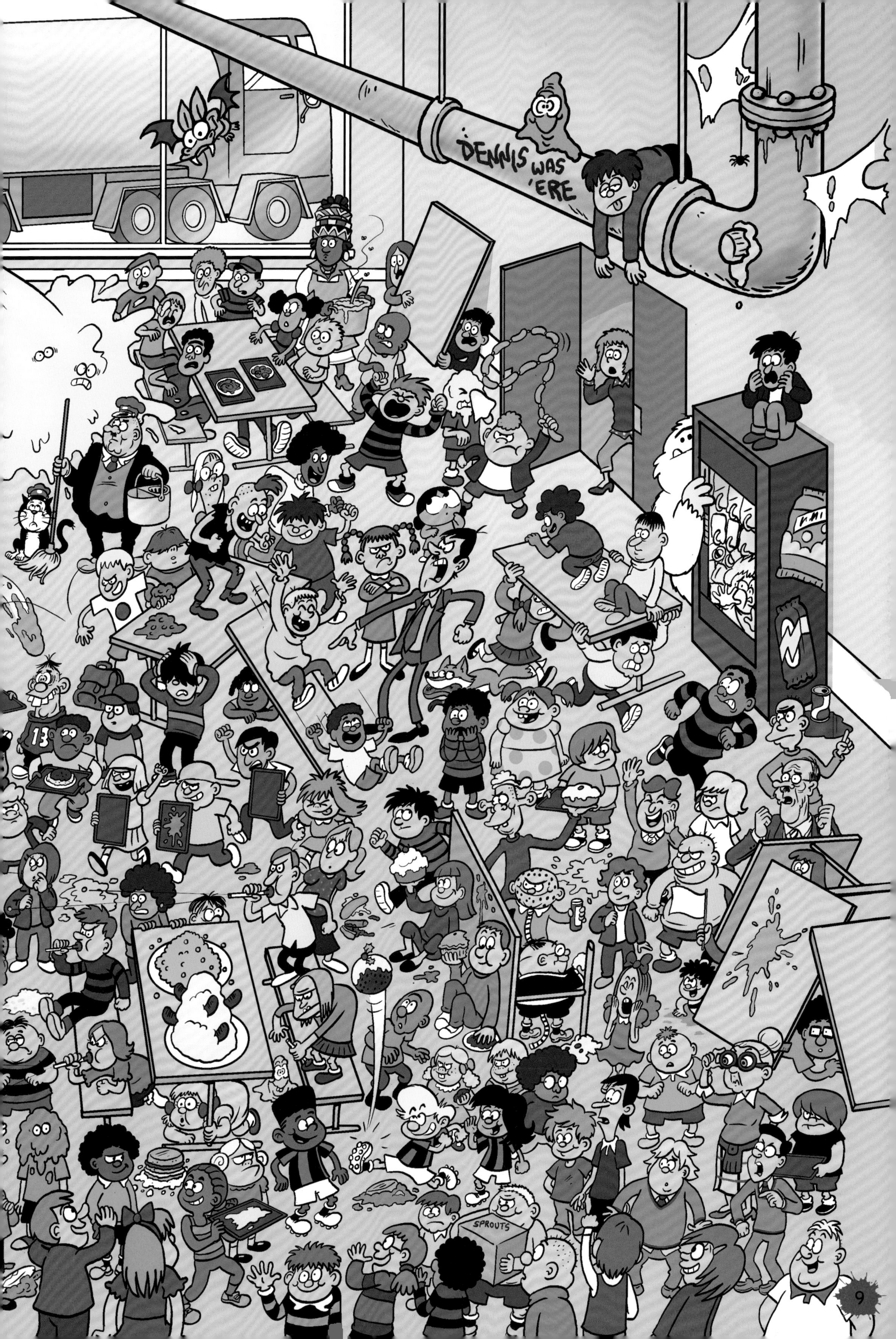

DENNIS WAS 'ERE
SPROUTS
13

Beanotown Tunnels

These tunnels are as mysterious as they are vast and run deep beneath Bash Street School. They hold many treasures and secrets: for example, the intriguing carvings on the cavern walls look like ancient Menace graffiti and there's a strangely familiar clockwork robot rampaging through the passageways. Perhaps Gnasher came down here to find a bone to gnaw on?

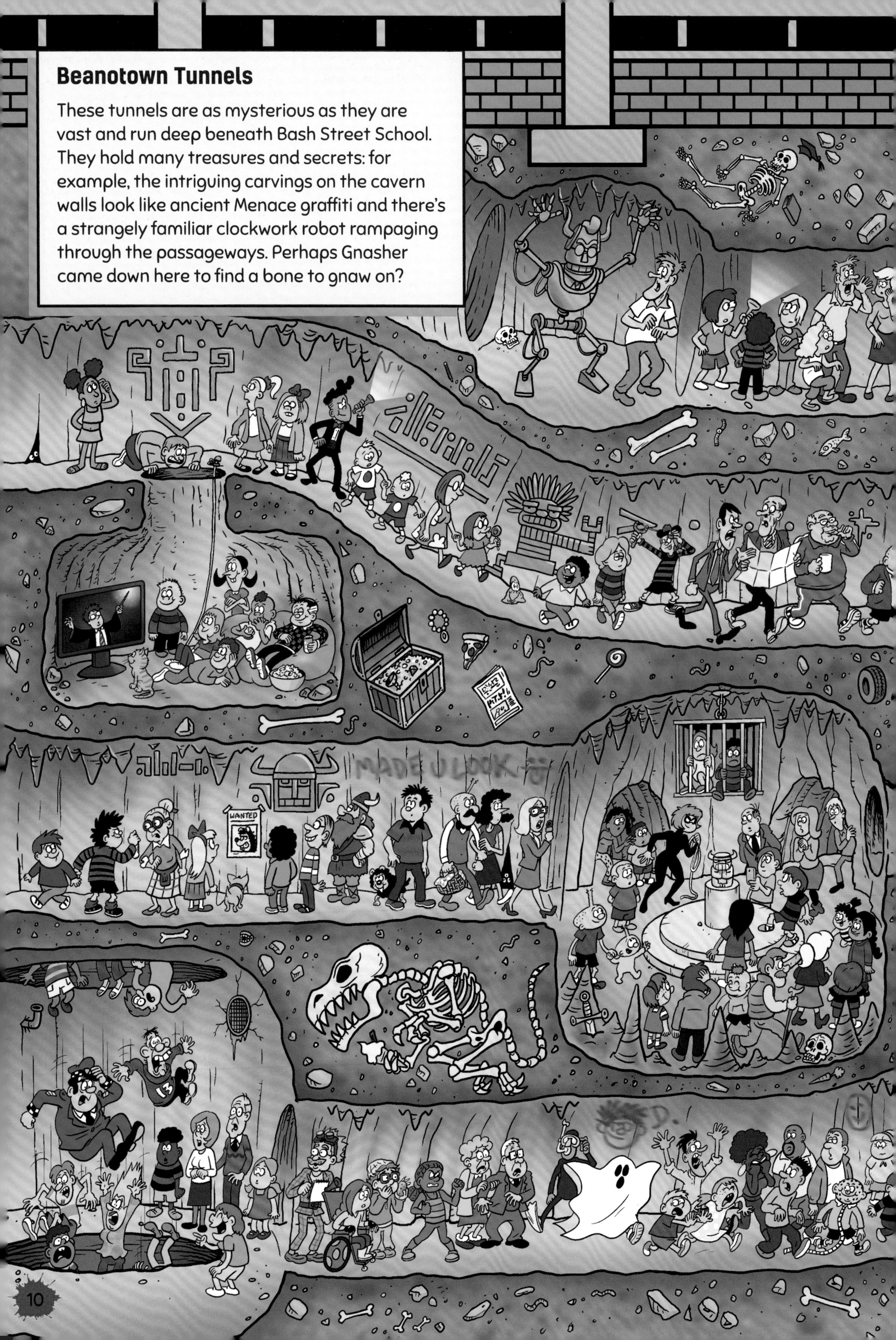
WANTED
MADE U LOOK
13

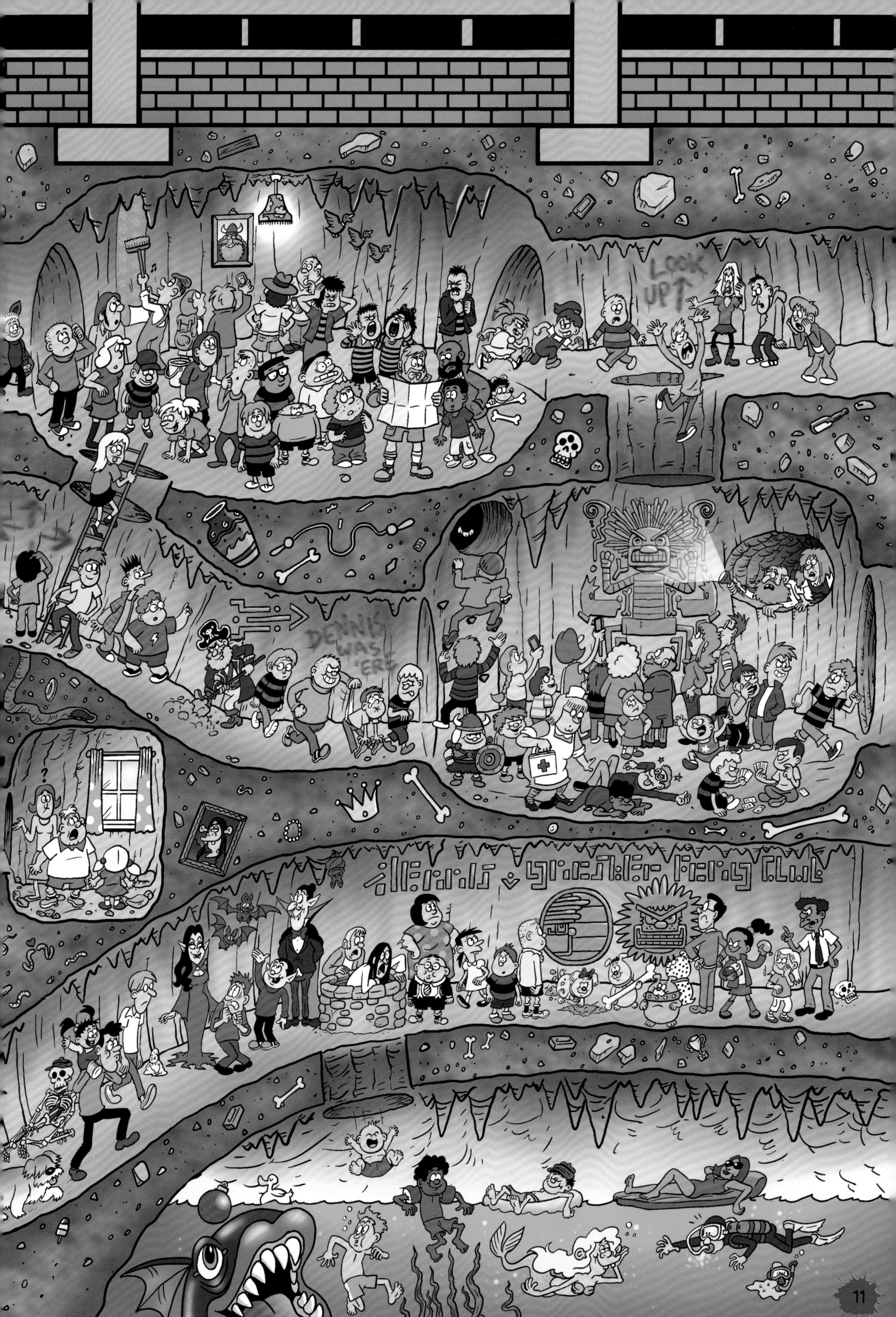
LOOK UP
DENNIS WAS 'ERE

Beanotown Park

This is the place to go for outdoor activities such as playing football, having water fights, going on the swings, discovering a Spring of Not Really Youth, being chased by a yeti in the woods . . . actually, maybe don't go into the woods. There's also been talk of a sausage-obsessed dog on the loose, stealing everyone's snacks and frisbees. Could it be Gnasher?

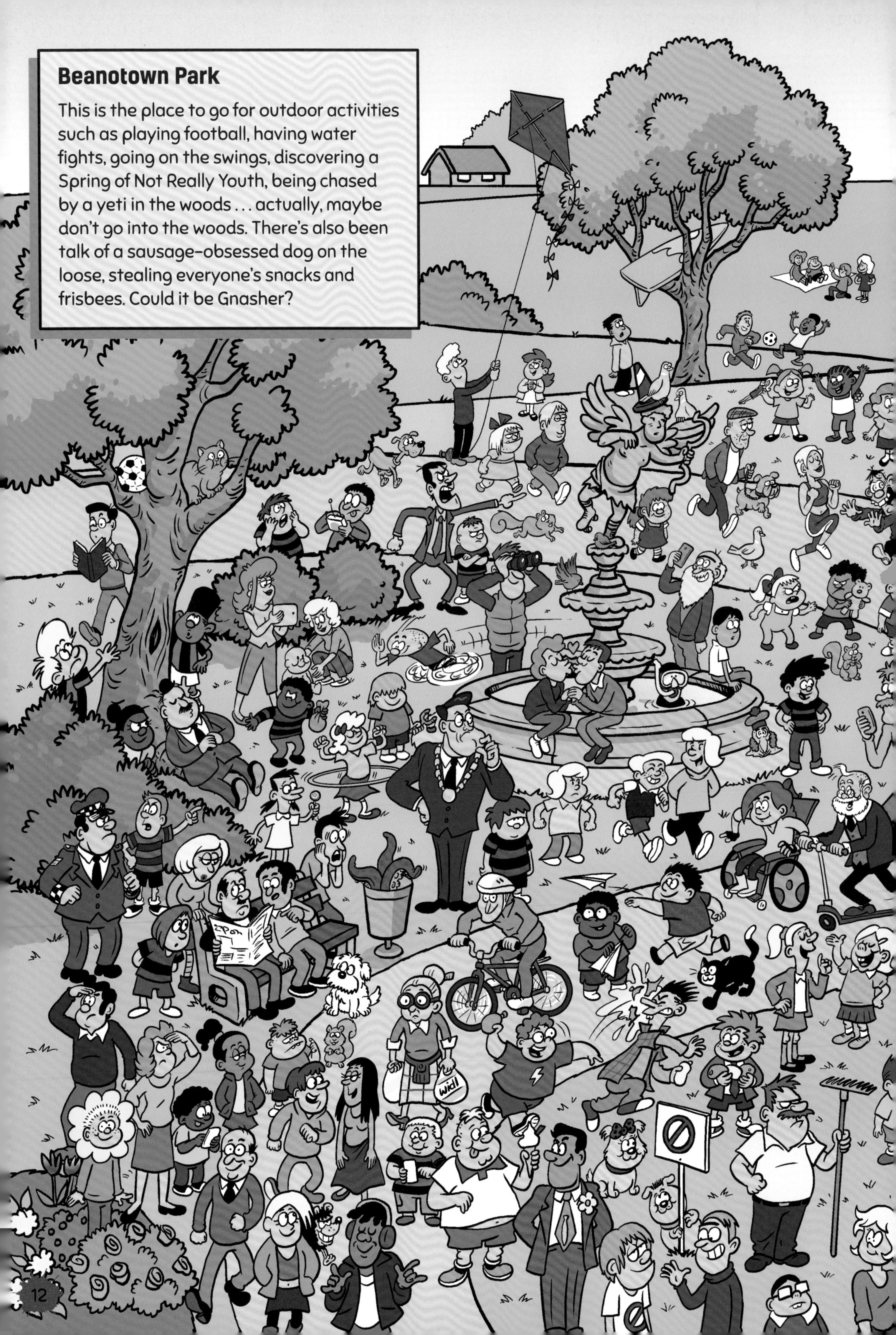
widl

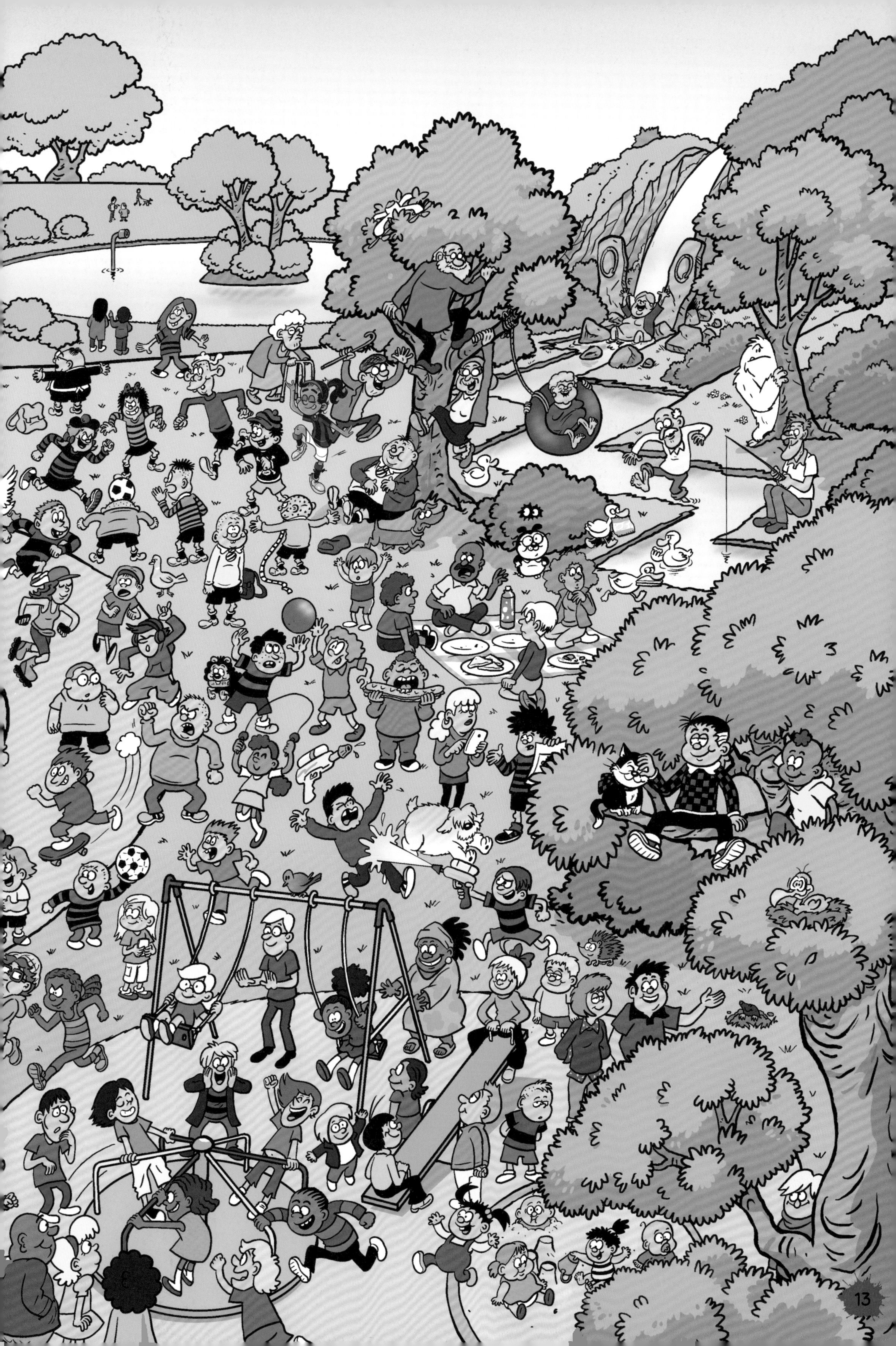

Duck Island

This is by far the strangest place in Beanotown, and that's really saying something. What appears to be a small island in the middle of the park's pond is actually an enormous land full of oddities. Watch out for the man-eating plants and, worse, dinosaurs – and whatever you do, do not insult the Vikings' hair. Basically, try not to die! And if you see Gnasher, tell him Dennis is looking for him.

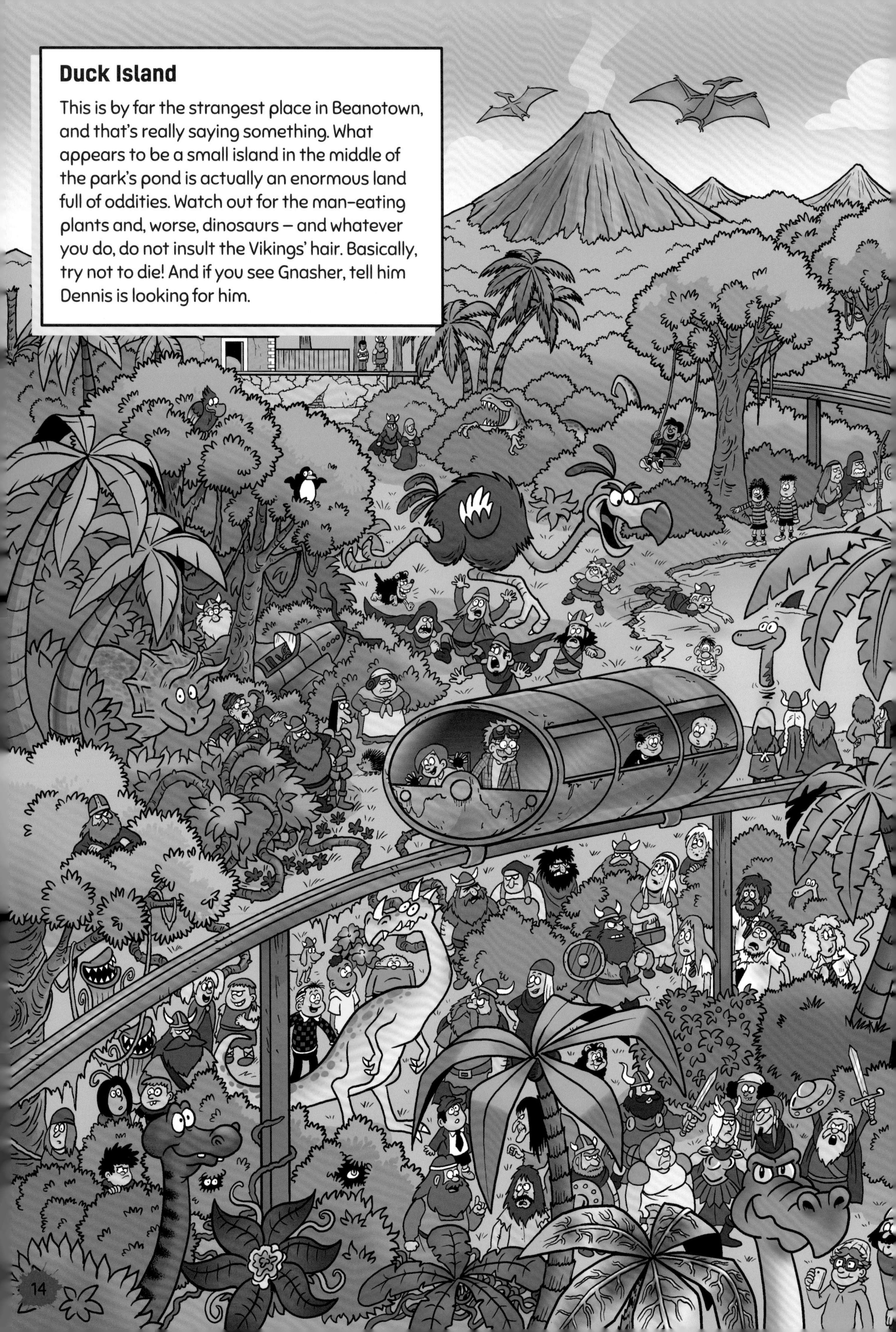

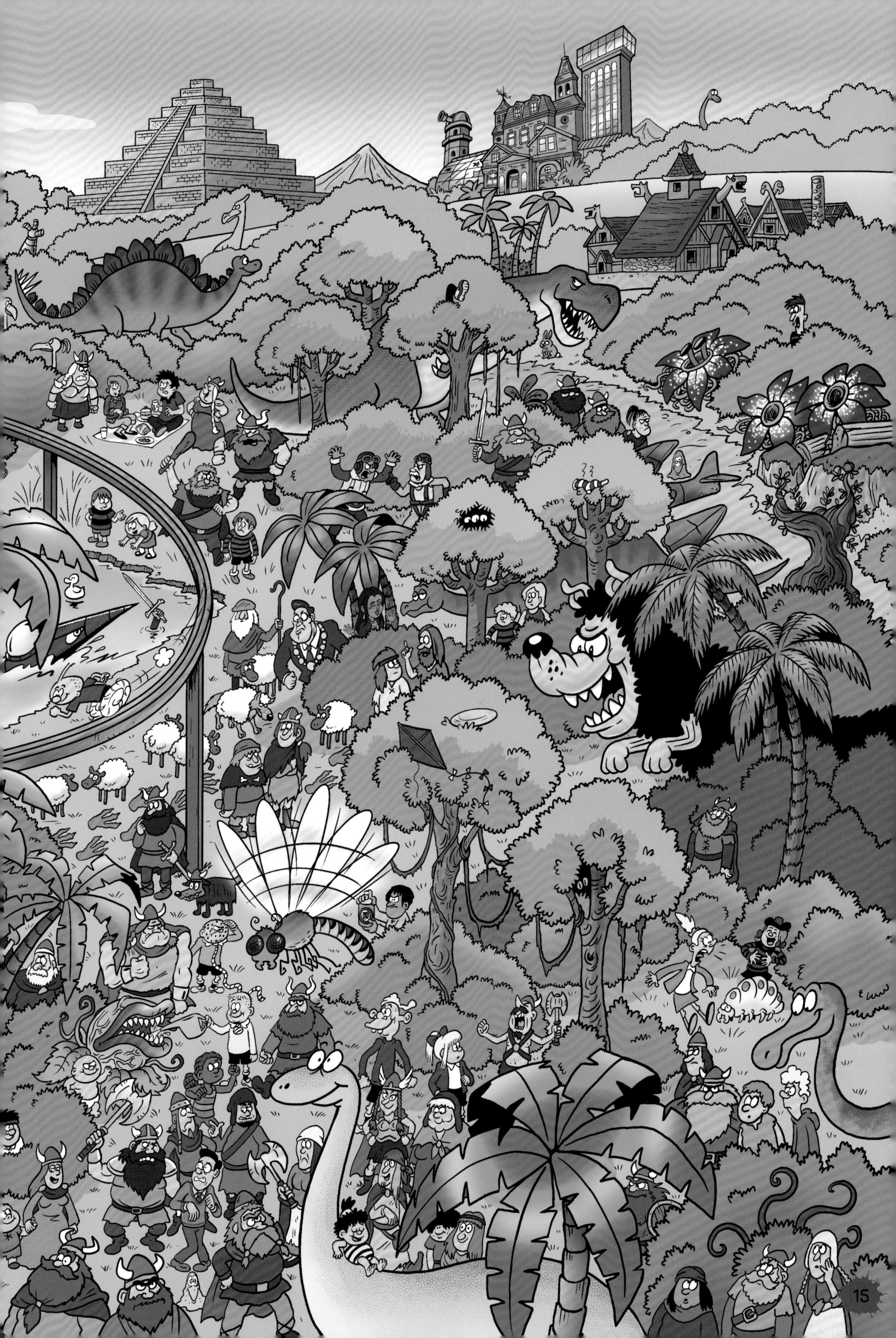

Beanotown High Street

This is not your average high street. If you want a new pair of shoes, a present for your gran or dishwasher tablets, then it's advised you go somewhere else. If you want the latest pranking gadget, the most sausage-y sausages or a stripy jumper, then Beanotown High Street has you covered. Now, where could Gnasher be hiding?

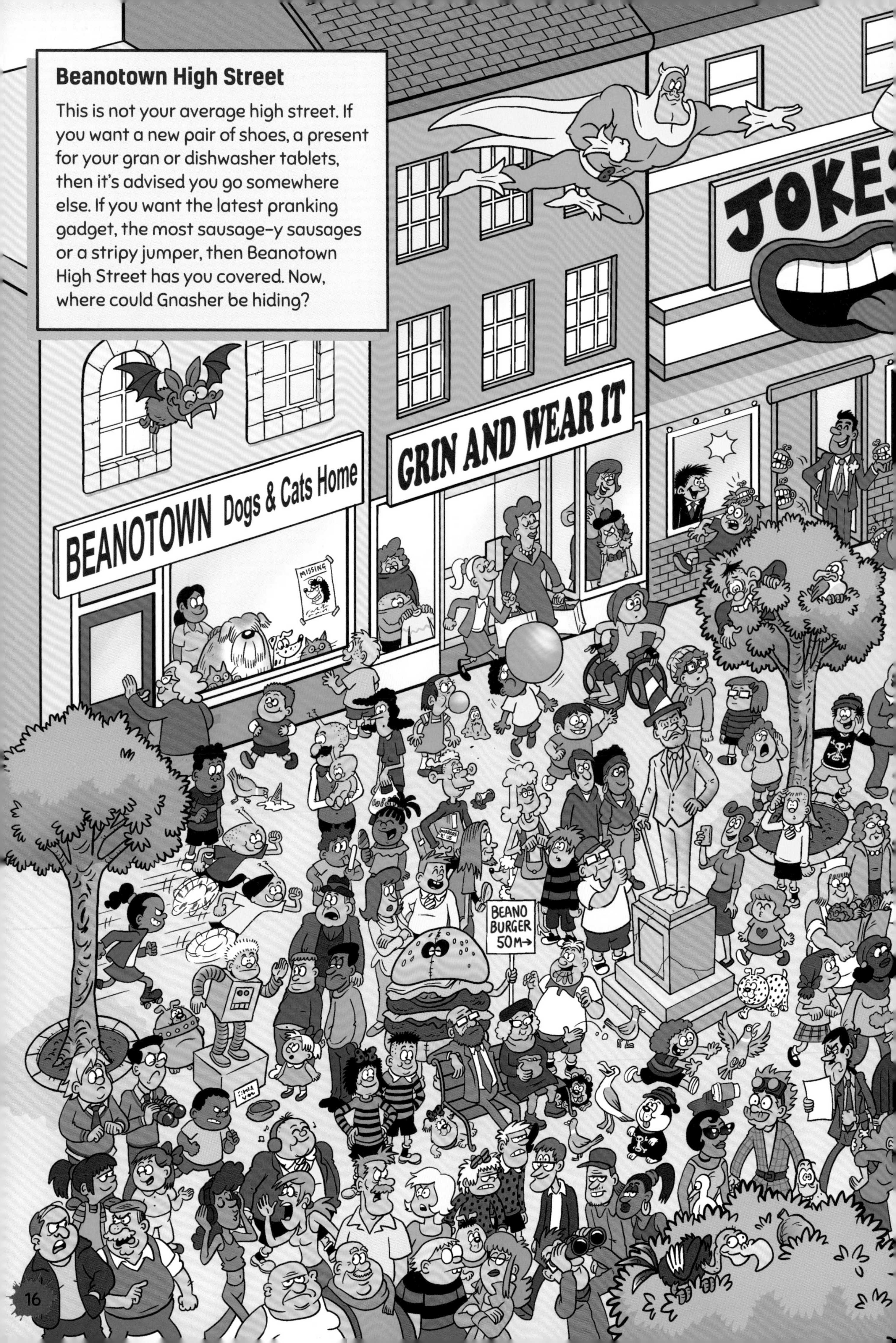
GRIN AND WEAR IT
BEANOTOWN Dogs & Cats Home
MISSING
BEANO BURGER 50M→

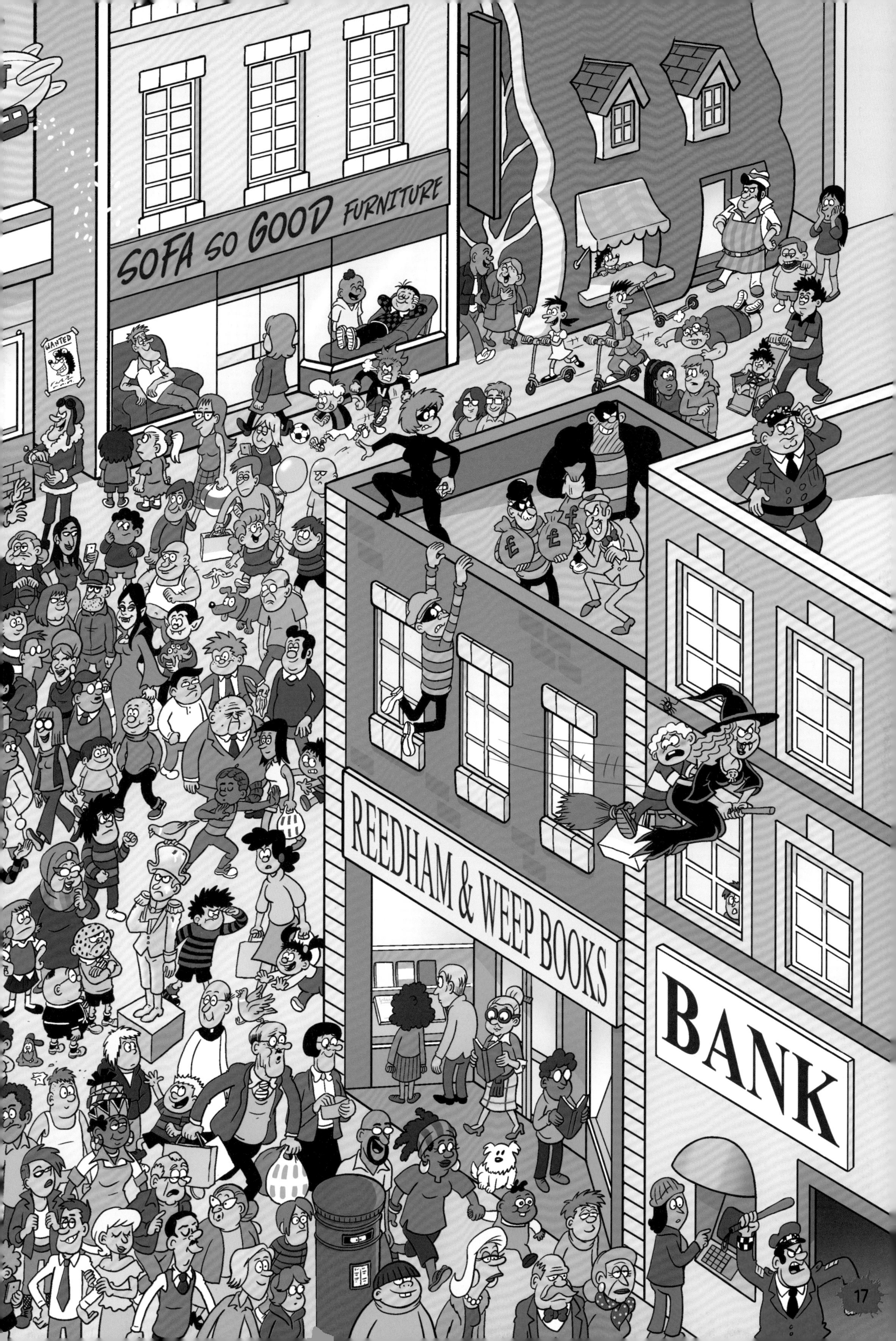
SOFA SO GOOD FURNITURE
WANTED
REEDHAM & WEEP BOOKS
BANK

Town Hall

Here is where Beanotown's policies and rules are made. For instance, Mayor Wilbur Brown's policy of no funkiness on Wednesdays, or of no funfairs in town, or of no fun whatsoever. Not many people know that the clock tower on top is a time machine. Perhaps Gnasher has gone and transported himself back in time? Let's hope we find him first!

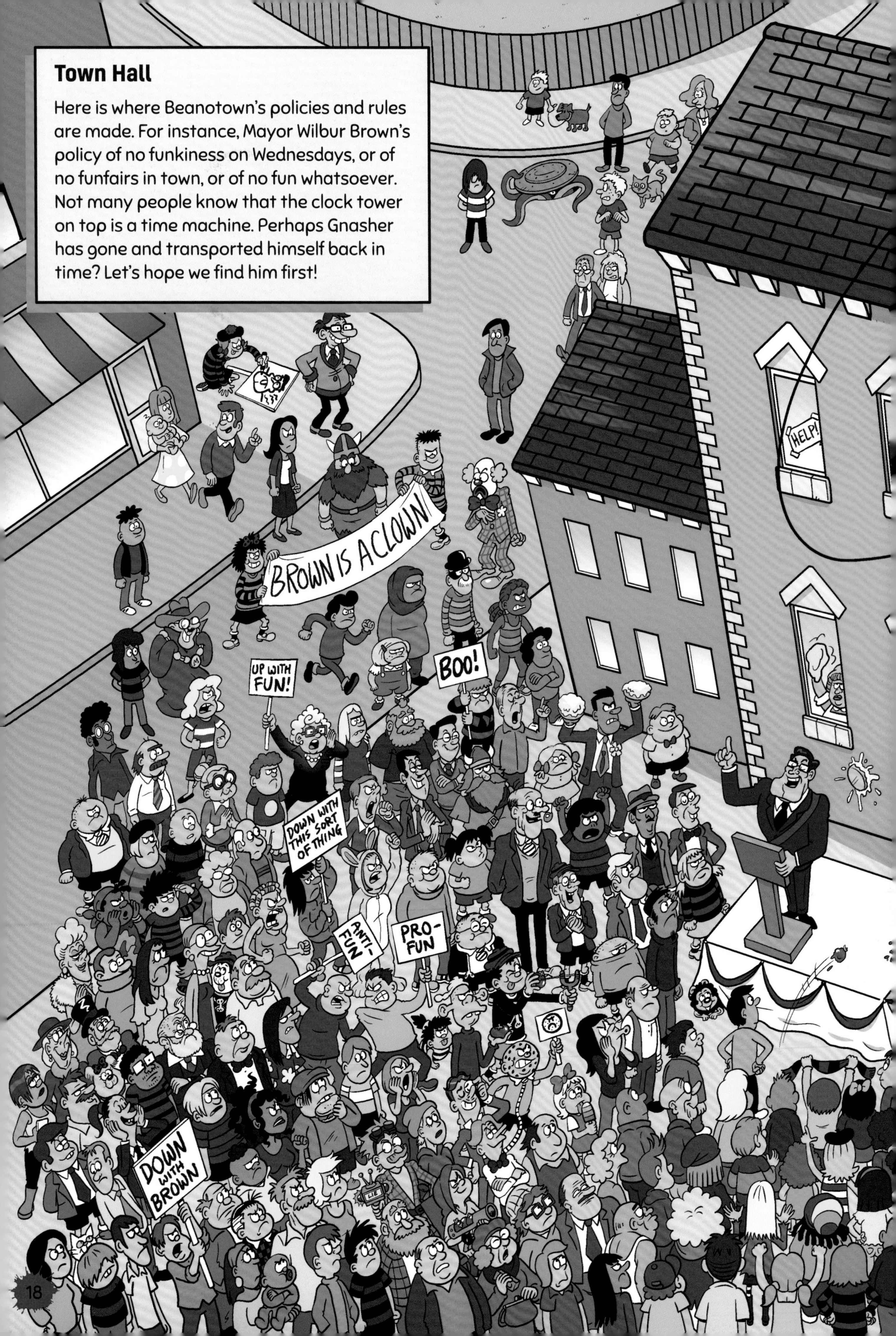
HELP!
BROWN IS A CLOWN
UP WITH FUN!
BOO!
DOWN WITH THIS SORT OF THING
ANTI-FUN
PRO-FUN
DOWN WITH BROWN
LIE

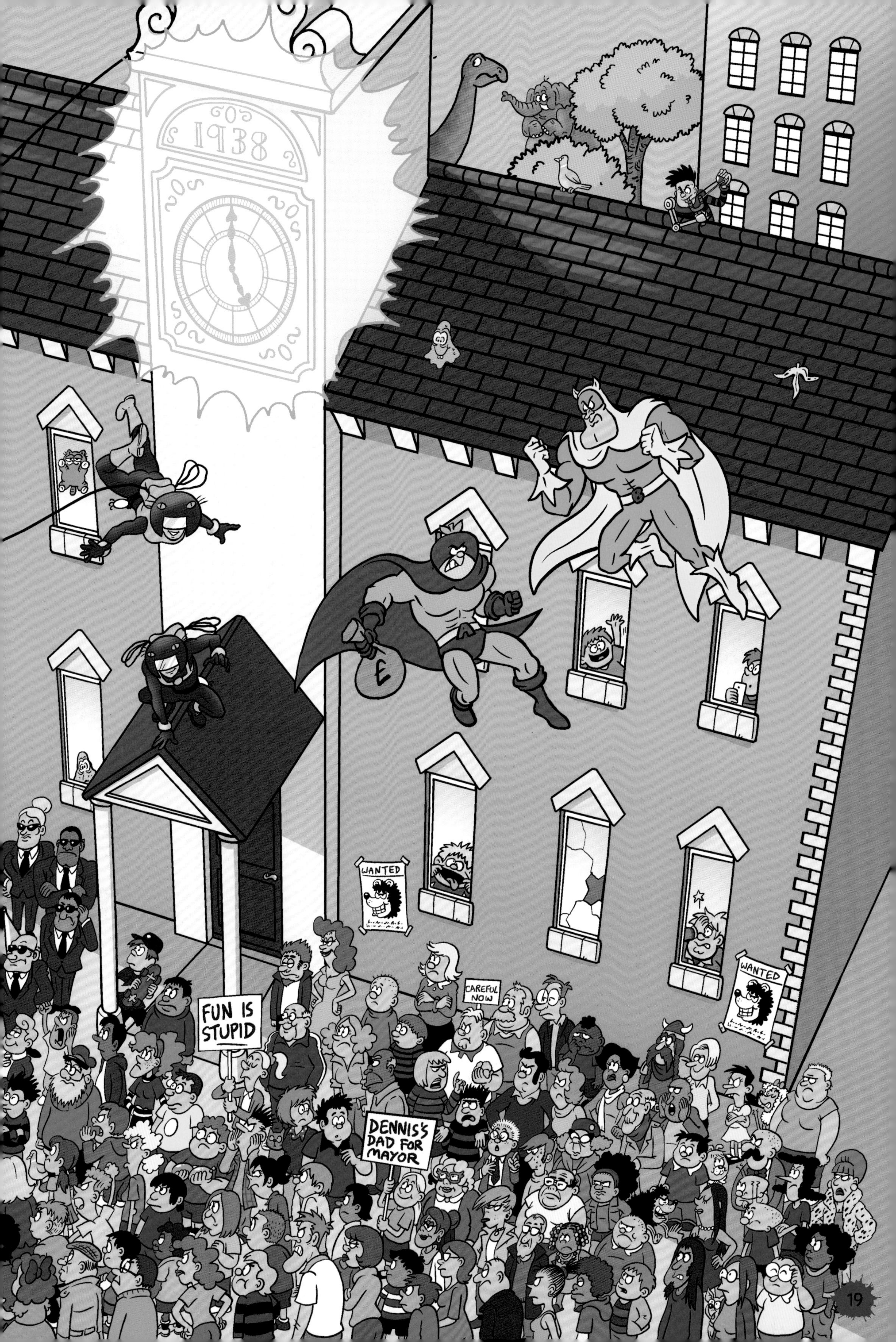
1938
WANTED
WANTED
CAREFUL NOW
FUN IS STUPID
DENNIS'S DAD FOR MAYOR

Beanotown Library

This is not your ordinary library. Though it certainly contains books, some of those books are a little . . . odd. Not to mention one of the librarians is a ghost! Beware of what you pull off the shelf – you might get more than you bargained for. If you're looking for Gnasher, I suggest you start at 'A' for animal.

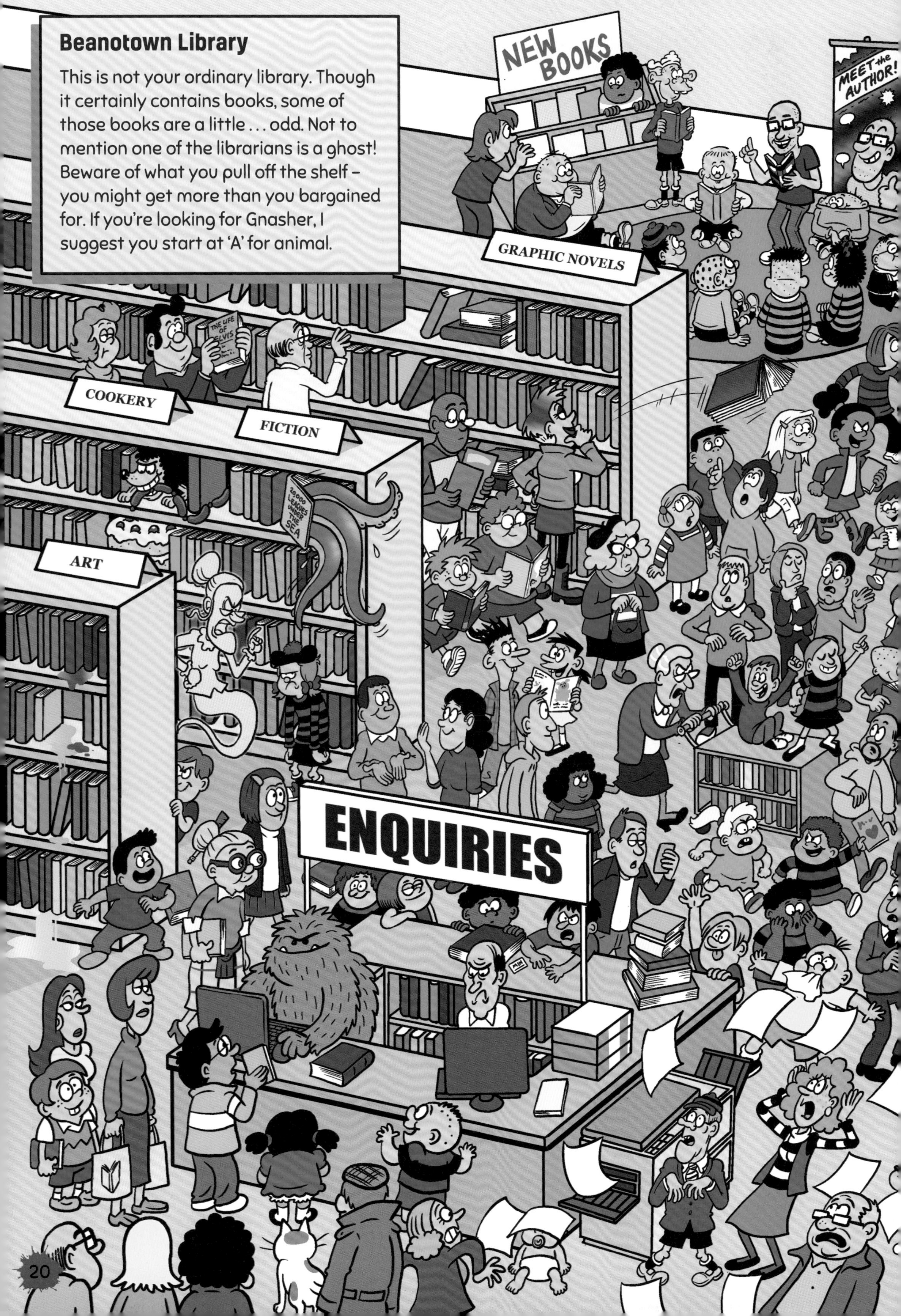

NEW BOOKS
MEET the AUTHOR!
GRAPHIC NOVELS
COOKERY
THE LIFE OF ELVIS
FICTION
20,000 LEAGUES UNDER THE SEA
ART
ENQUIRIES

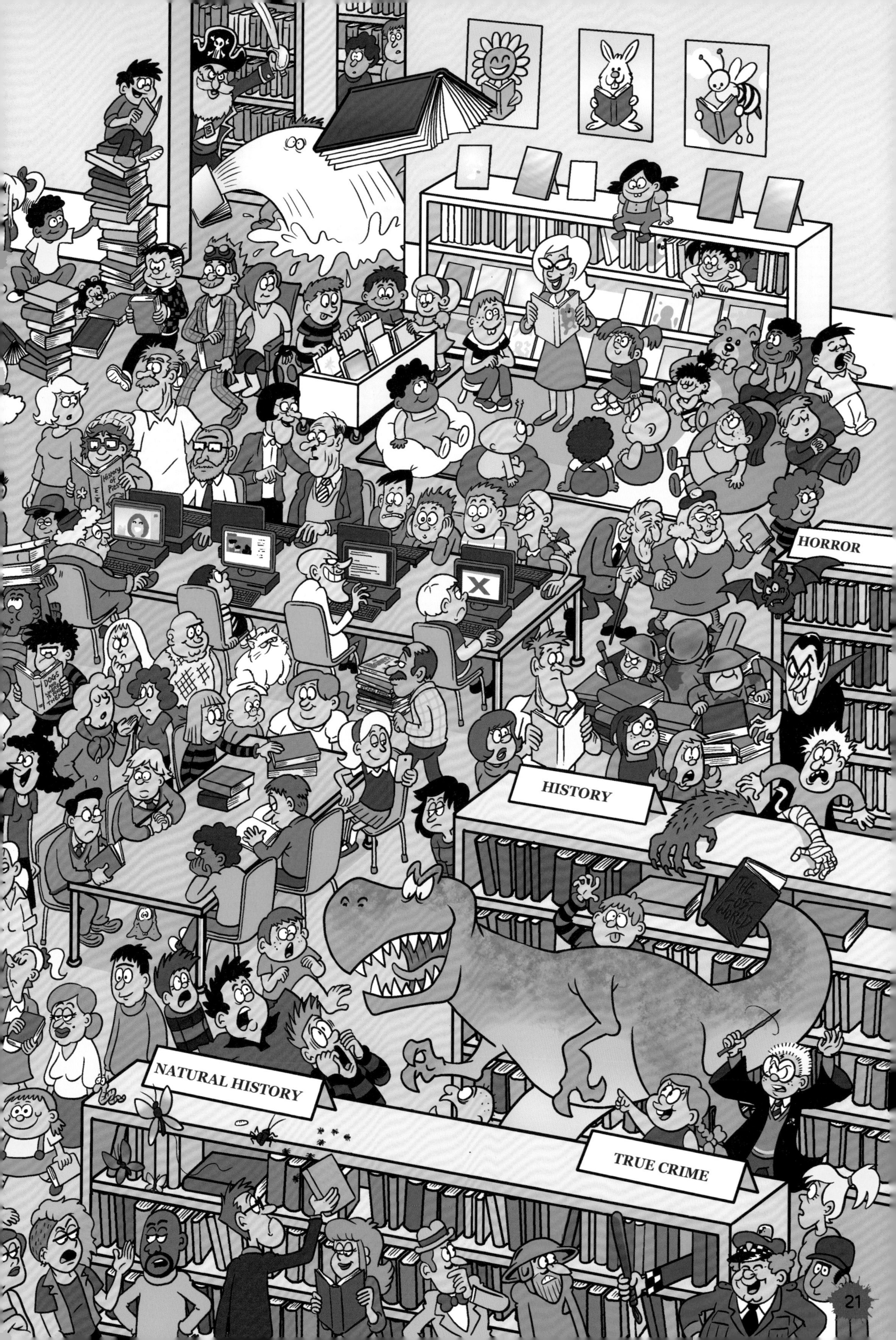
History of Pies
DOGS AND WHERE TO FIND THEM
HORROR
HISTORY
THE LOST WORLD
NATURAL HISTORY
TRUE CRIME

Beanotown Museum

This museum is as confusing as it is educational. Sure, it has historical artefacts and those little plaques with tiny writing telling you about what the object is, where it was found, blah, blah blah, blah blah . . . but the exhibits are all quite unusual. Must-sees include Thor's toothpick and a copy of the very first Beano annual! Among all this strangeness, can you spot Gnasher?

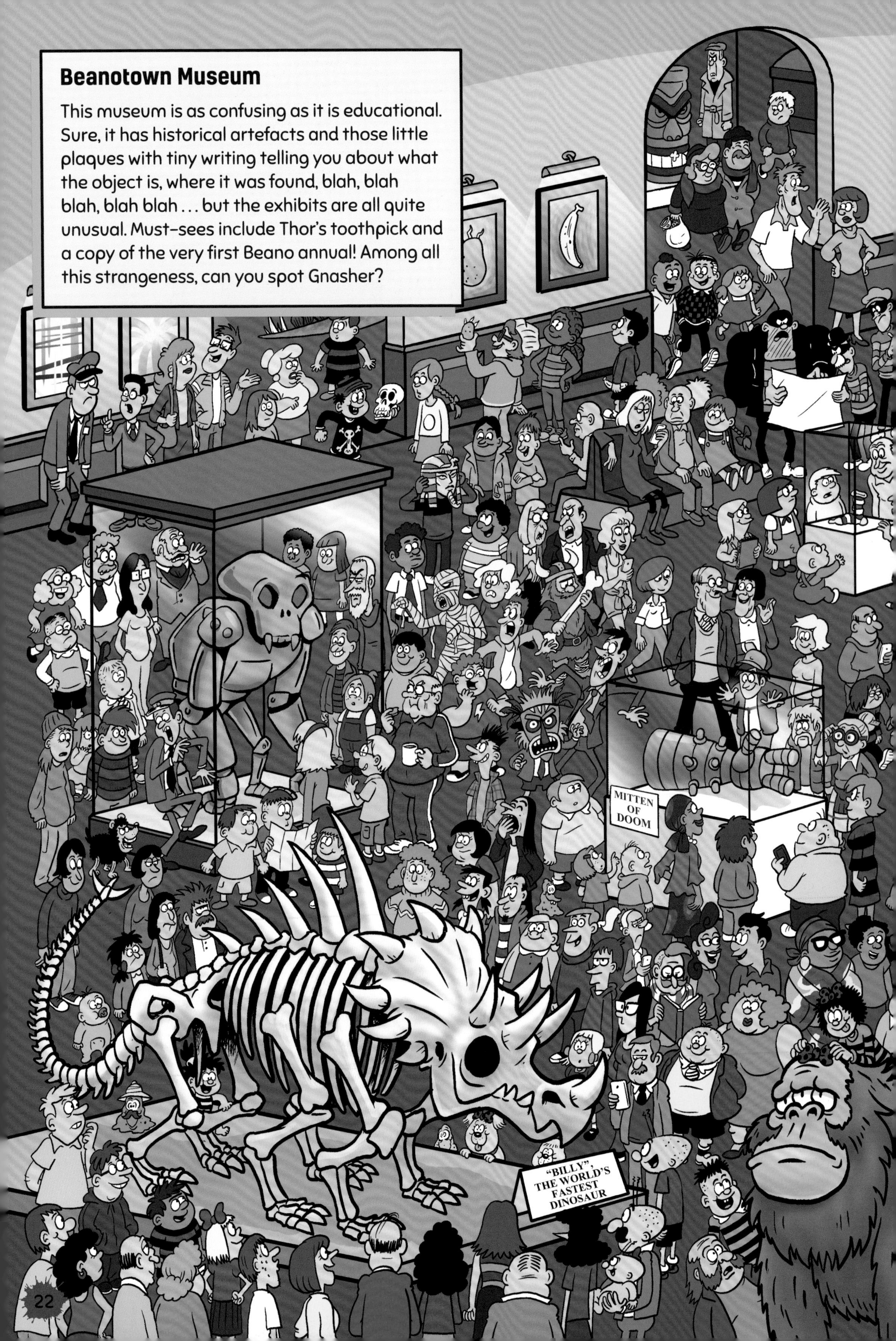
MITTEN OF DOOM
"BILLY", THE WORLD'S FASTEST DINOSAUR

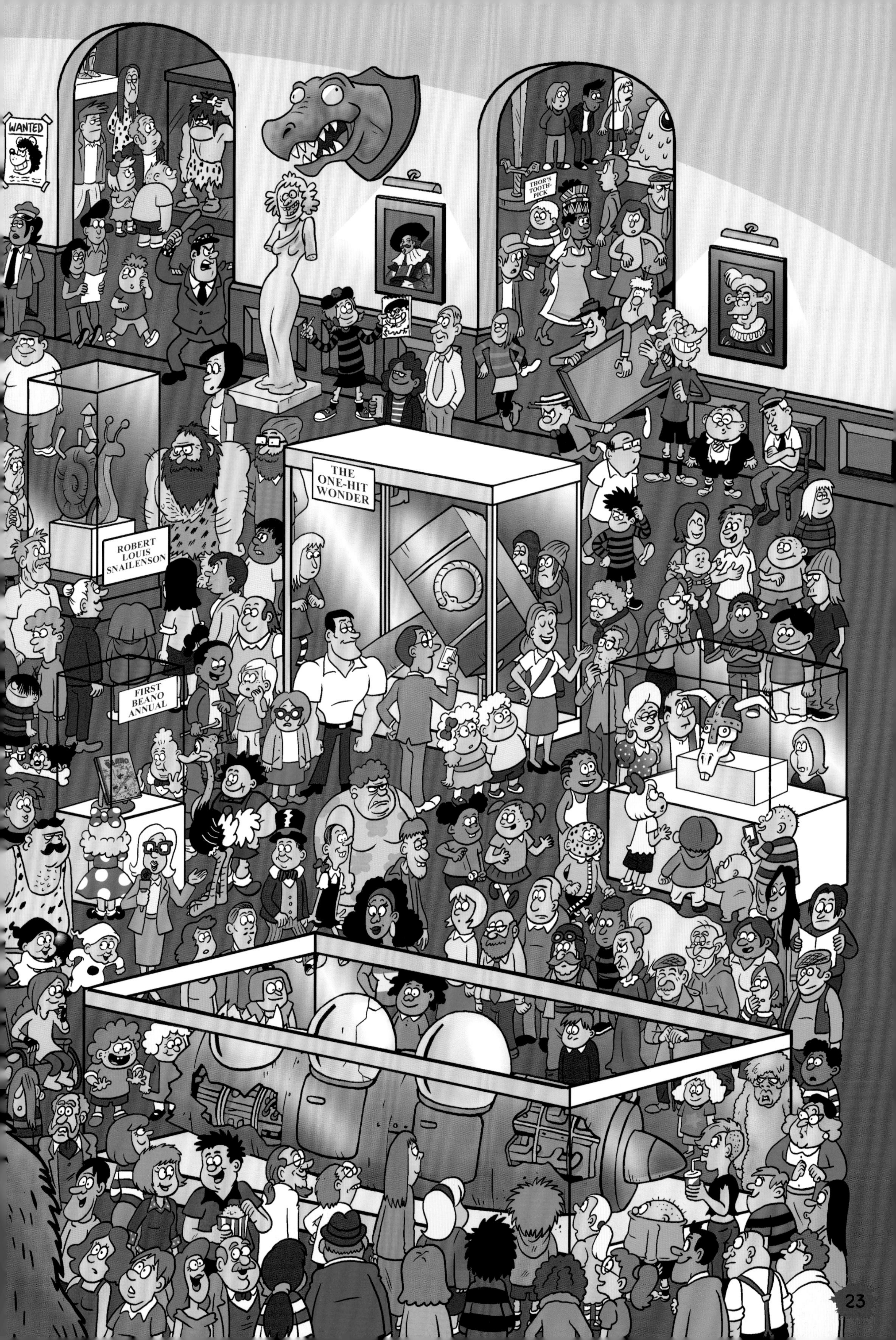
WANTED
THOR'S TOOTH-PICK
THE ONE-HIT WONDER
ROBERT LOUIS SNAILENSON
FIRST BEANO ANNUAL

Horrible Hall

Believe it or not, this was once Beanotown's school, before it was destroyed. Dennis's gran even received her education there! Legend says that the Headless Headmaster haunts Horrible Hall (try saying that quickly three times while standing on one leg), but seeing is believing. It's Halloween and everyone is in costume. Can you see what Gnasher is dressed as?

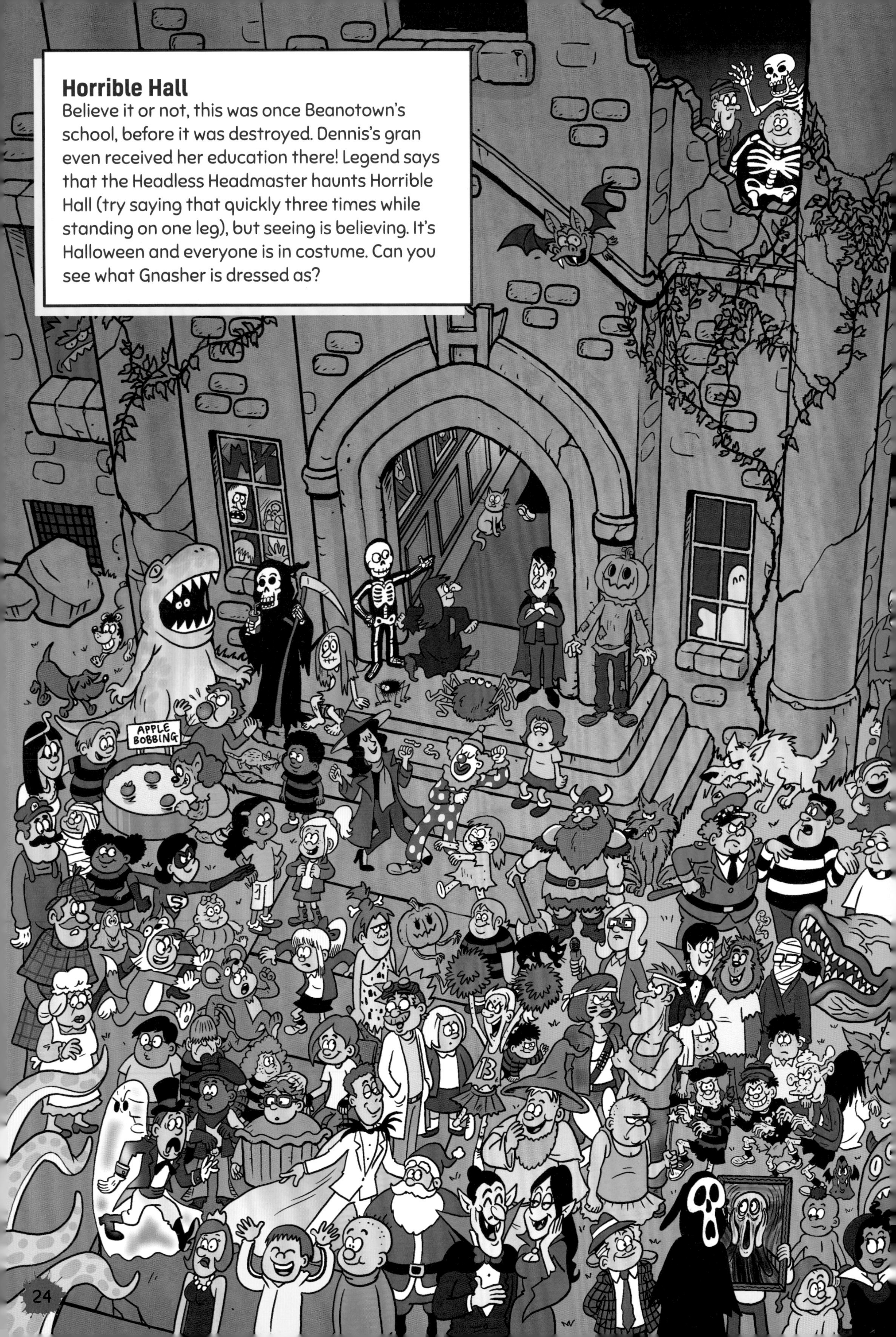

APPLE BOBBING
13

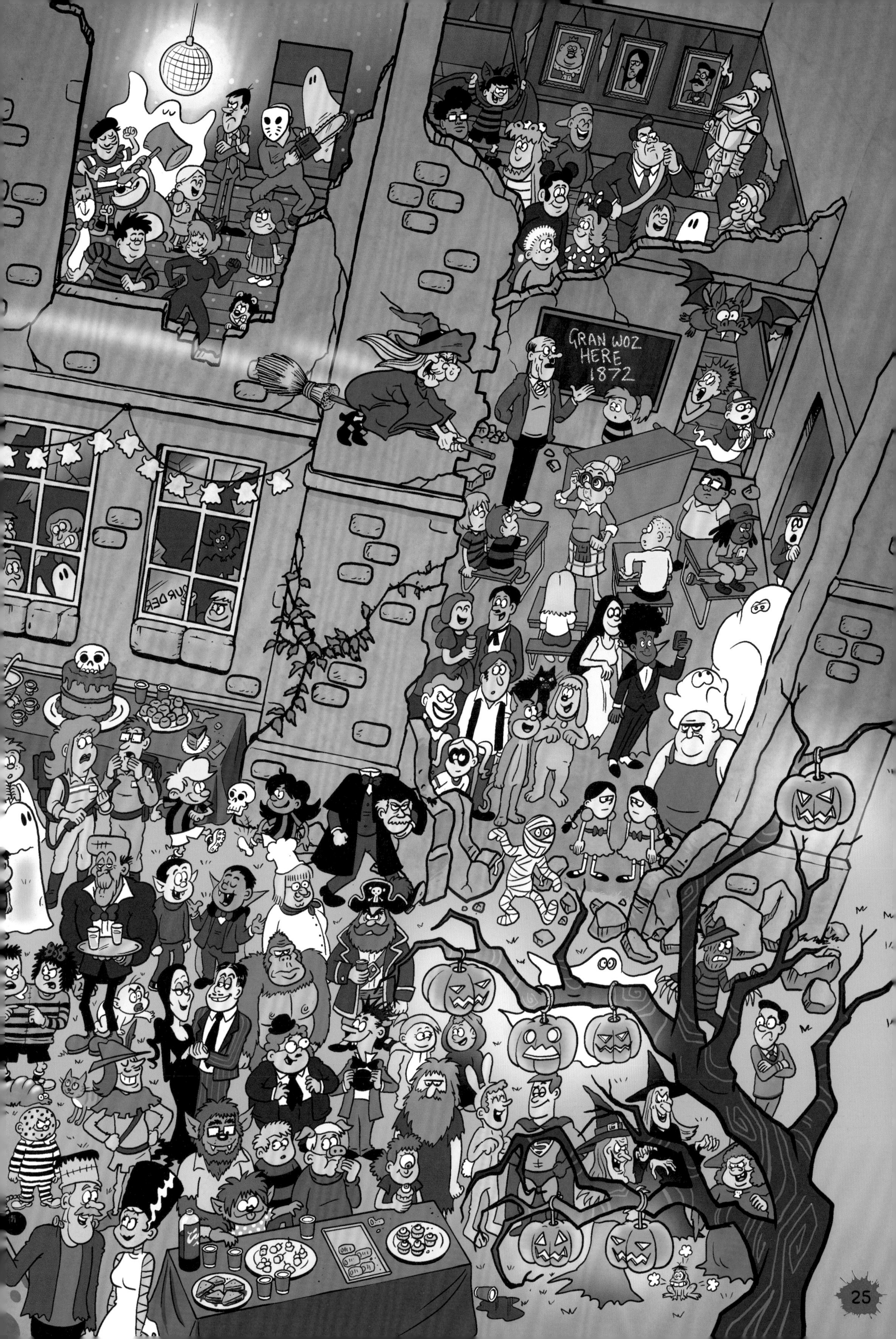
GRAN WOZ HERE 1872

Mount Beano

This mighty, snow-capped peak offers the citizens of Beanotown year-round skiing, as it has its own microclimate, which means it even snows in the middle of a heatwave! This is great for Mr Frosty the snowman, but isn't such great news for Dennis, who is still looking for Gnasher. Surely he'll be easy to spot against all that white snow though!

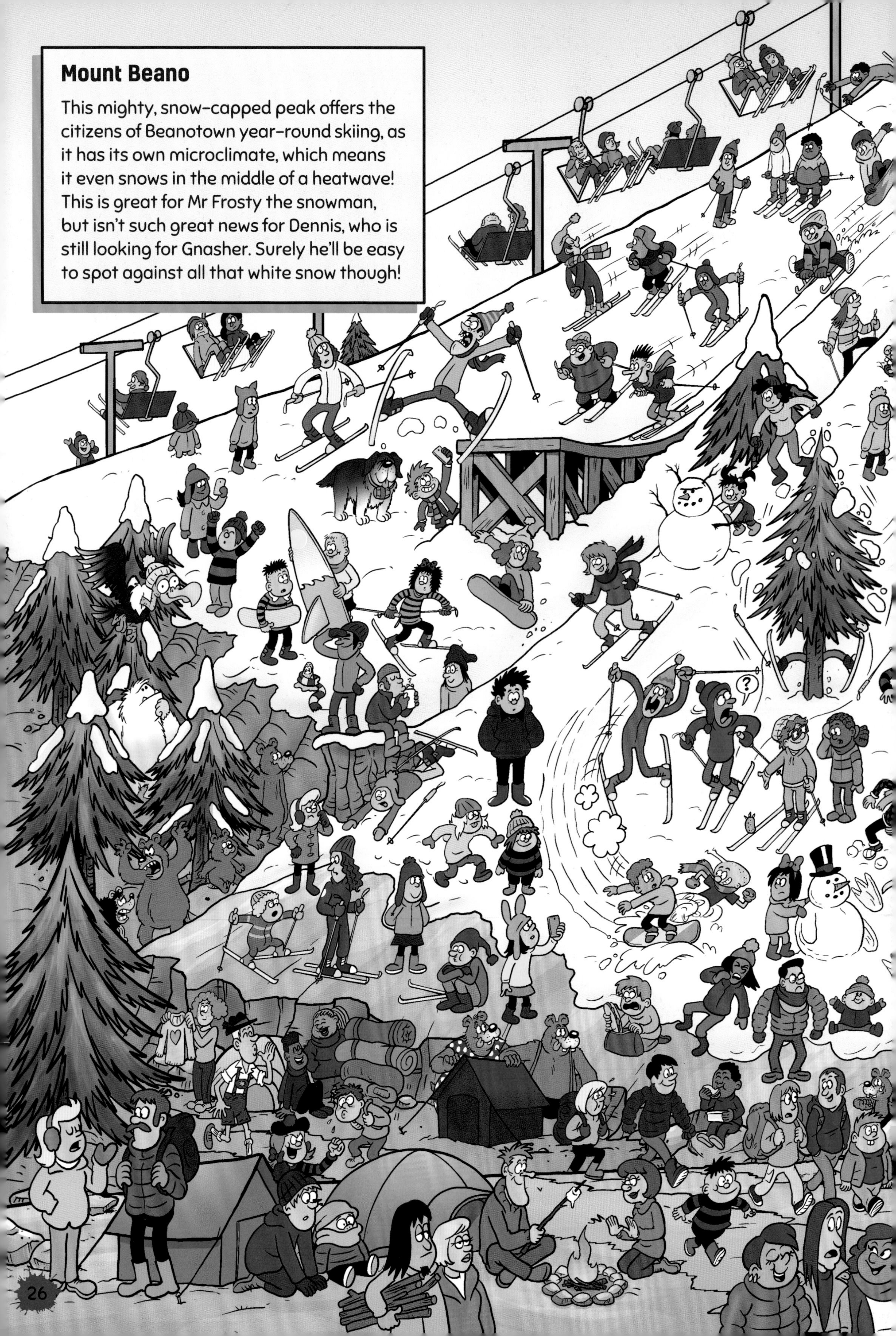

?

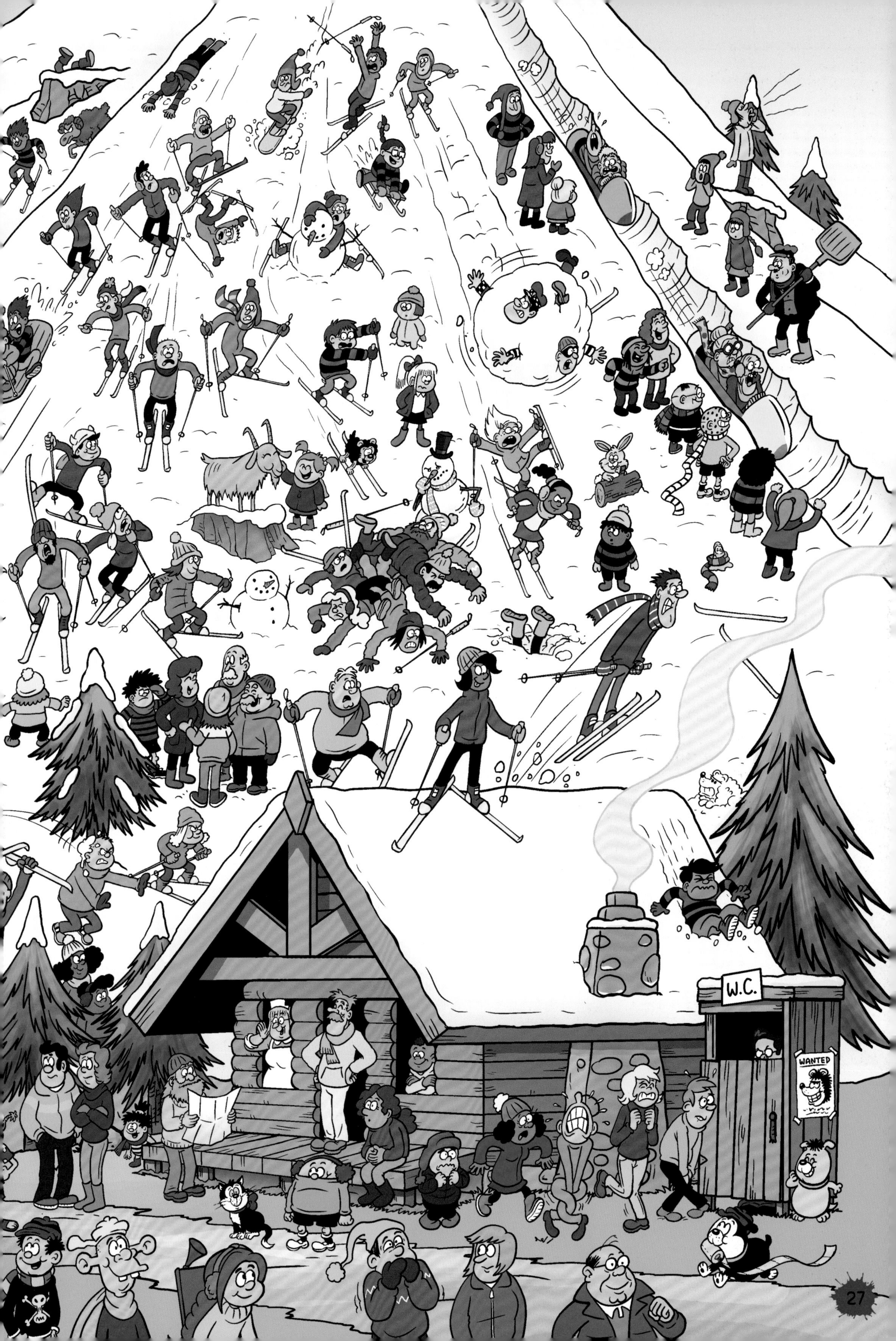
W.C.
WANTED

Beanotown Zoo

The zoo and its keepers are leaders in animal conservation. It's just a shame that they can't seem to conserve the animals within their enclosures! There are daily escapes, and the citizens of Beanotown have become used to seeing an elephant strolling past their living room windows, or a troop of monkeys swinging by the greengrocer's. Maybe Gnasher is hiding here, looking for a new furry friend.

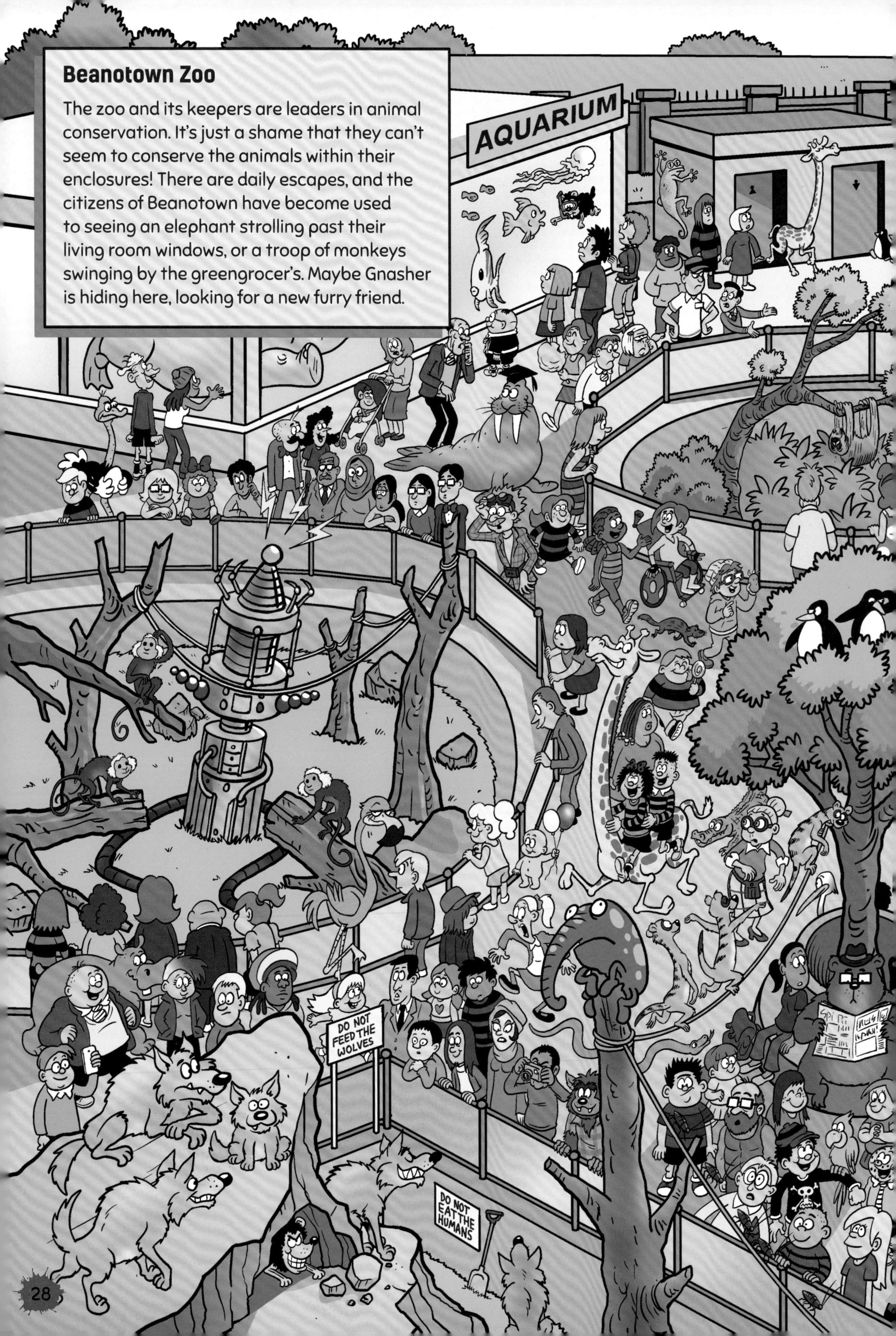

AQUARIUM
DO NOT FEED THE WOLVES
DO NOT EAT THE HUMANS

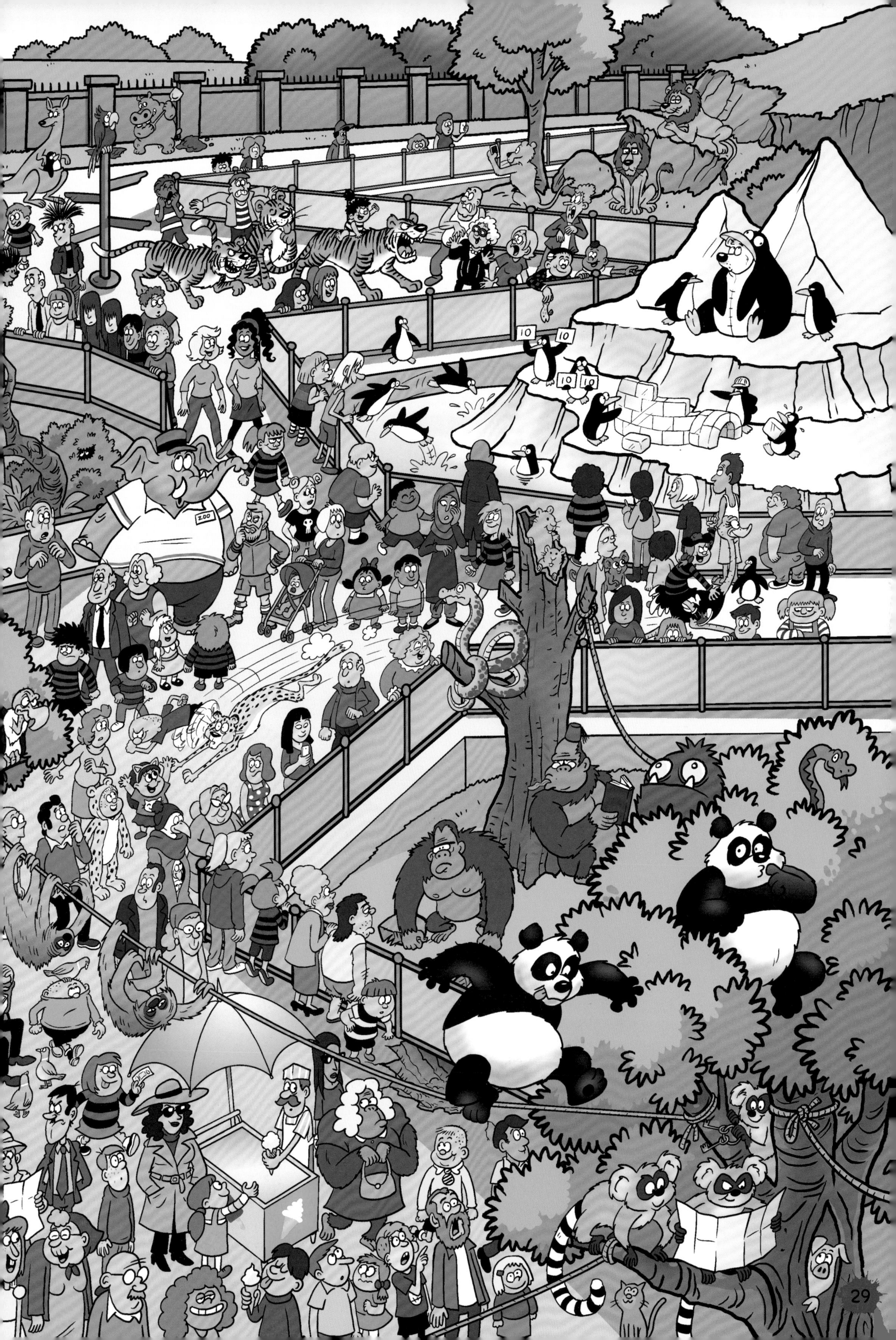
10
10
10
10
ZOO

Beanotown-on-Sea

This isn't quite the postcard-worthy seaside escape you'd hope for, but there is sea and sand for those who love a splash or sunbathe. Be wary of what lurks beneath the waves, however, as there's more than just the occasional jellyfish down there. It looks as though someone has spotted Dennis at least, for the black lighthouse light is on ... but where is Gnasher?

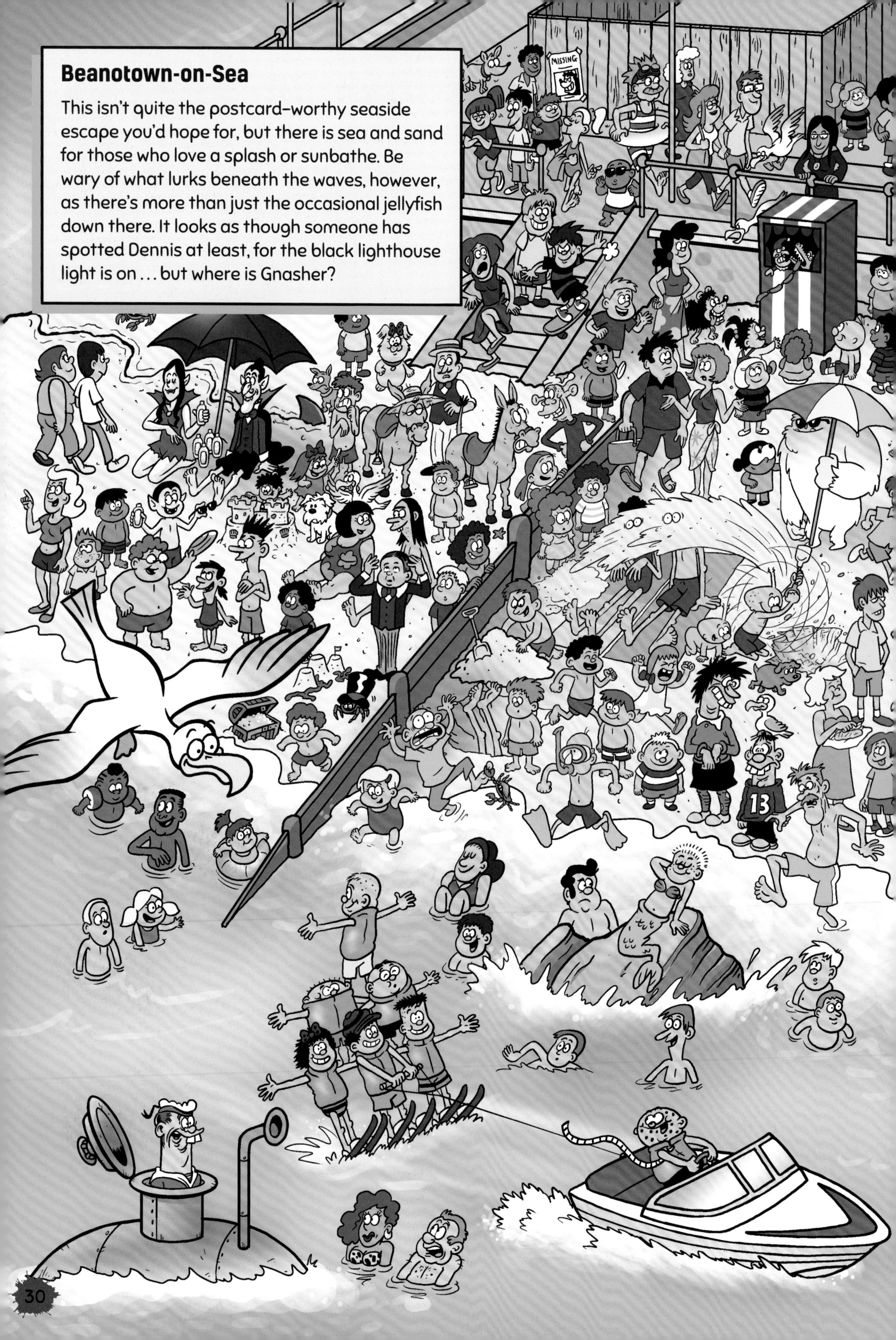

MISSING
13

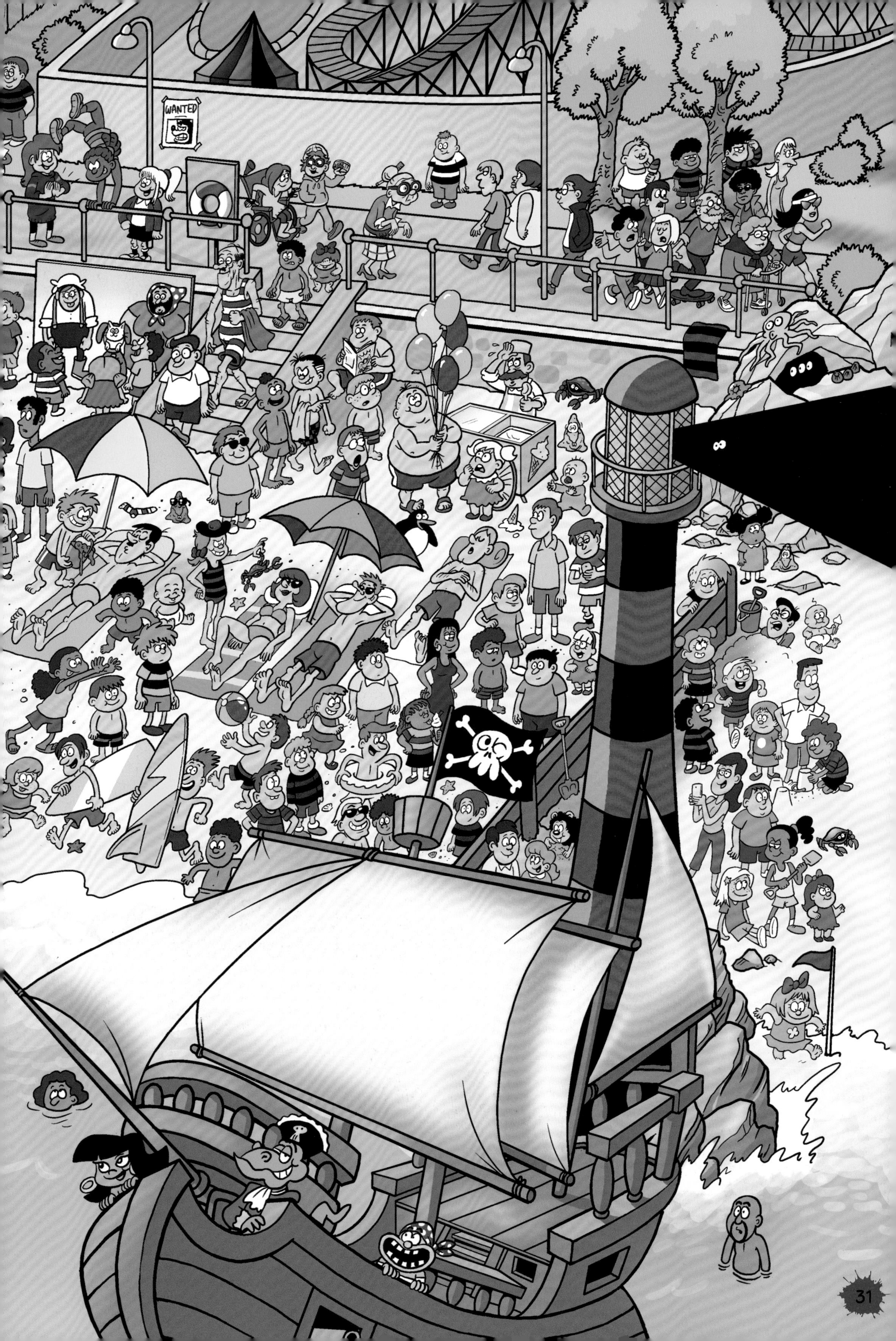
WANTED

Beanotown Police Station

This is where you'll find the sneakiest, meanest characters Beanotown has to offer – and that's just the police officers! You might also meet some hardened criminals, such as General Blight and Dr Gloom, locked up in the cells. It looks like Gnasher's trail has led us all the way here, but can you spot him and reunite Dennis with his best friend?

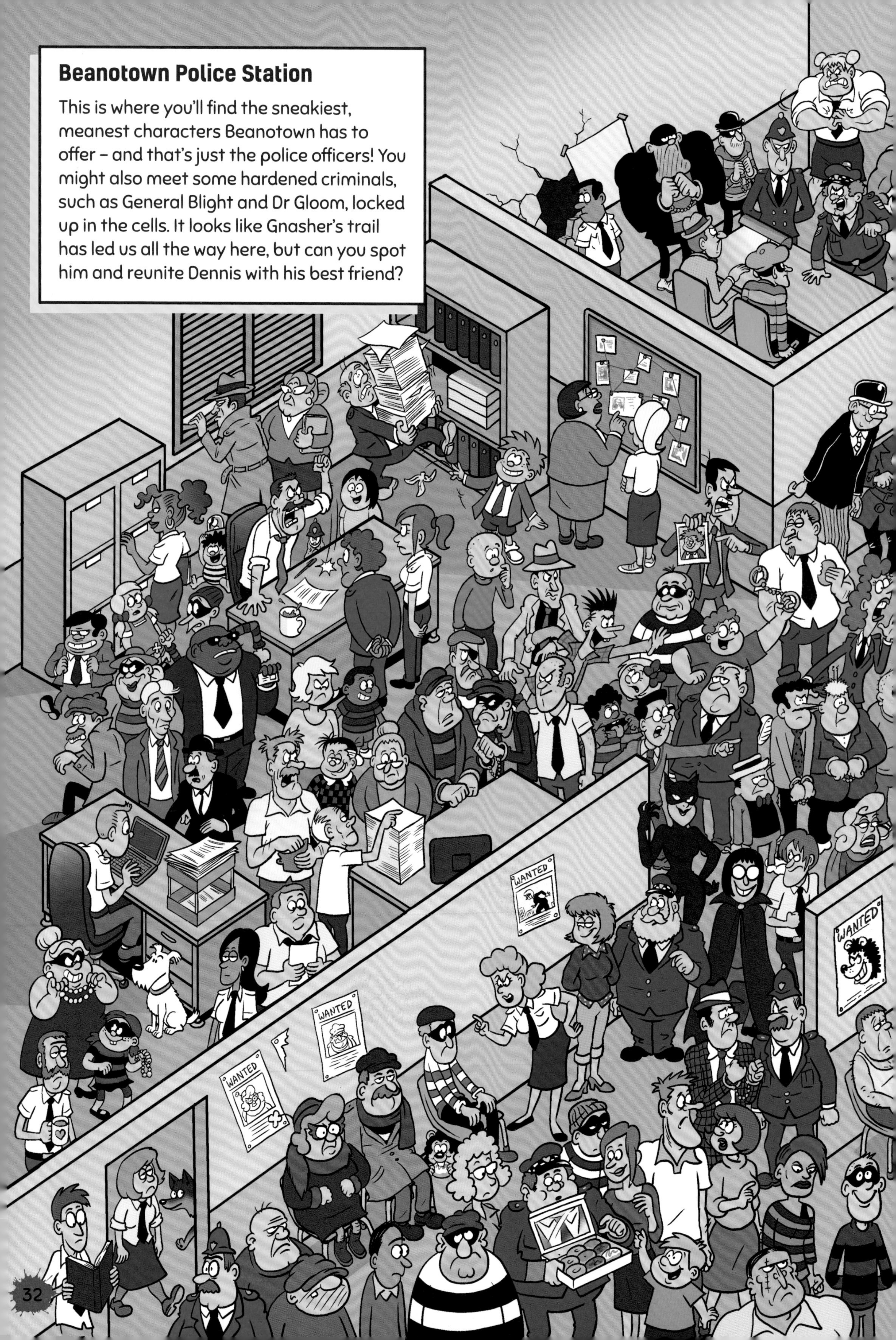
WANTED
WANTED
WANTED
WANTED

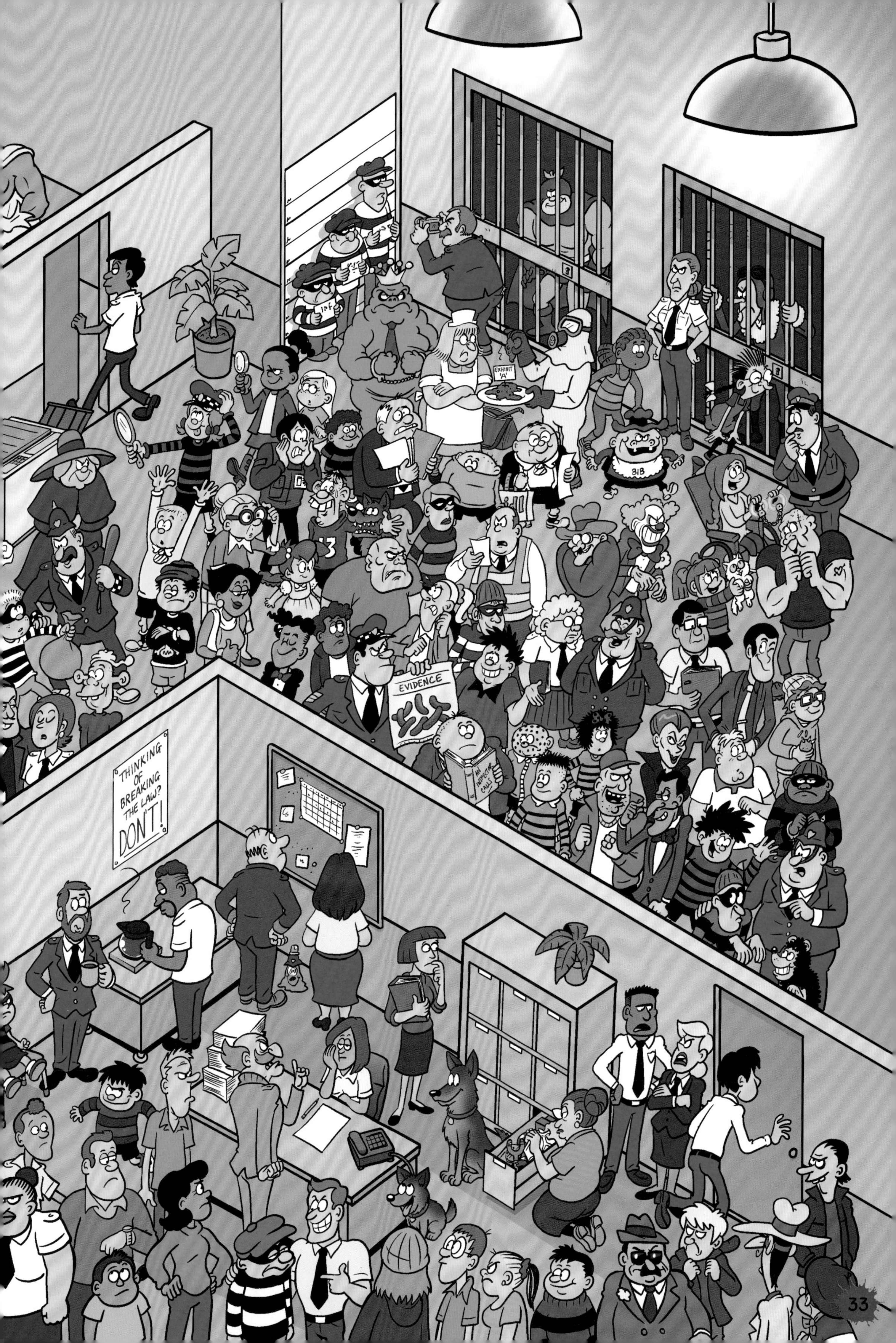
EXHIBIT 'A'
BIB
EVIDENCE
AN INSPECTOR CALLS
THINKING OF BREAKING THE LAW? DON'T!

WANT MORE FUN?

Try finding these hidden characters and objects!

p06 – 51 Gasworks Road

- ☐ Dennis Senior
- ☐ Sandra Menace
- ☐ A black-and-red wrapped present
- ☐ Sergeant Slipper
- ☐ A gnome with a green hat
- ☐ A pink cupcake

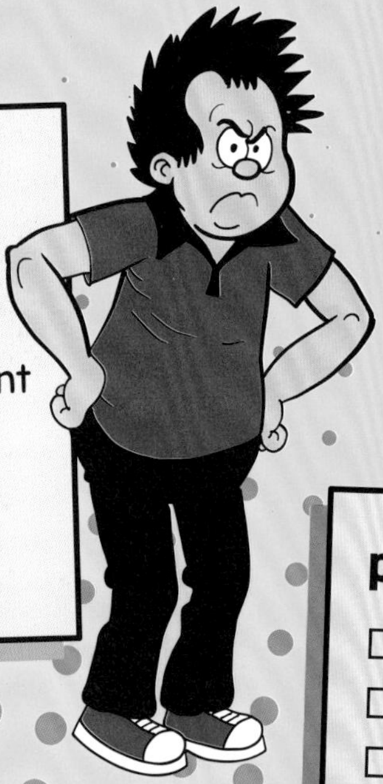

p08 – Bash Street School

- ☐ Mr Teacher
- ☐ A green squelchy
- ☐ A science book
- ☐ Olive Spratt
- ☐ Olive Pratt
- ☐ A red rucksack

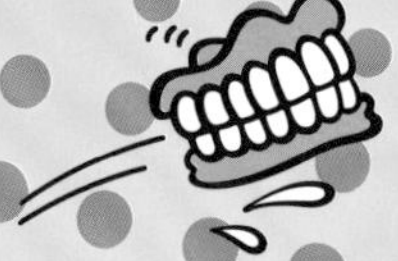

p10 – Beanotown Tunnels

- ☐ A golden peashooter
- ☐ A lost snorkeller
- ☐ A Viking Shield
- ☐ Calamity James
- ☐ A pirate
- ☐ A set of false teeth

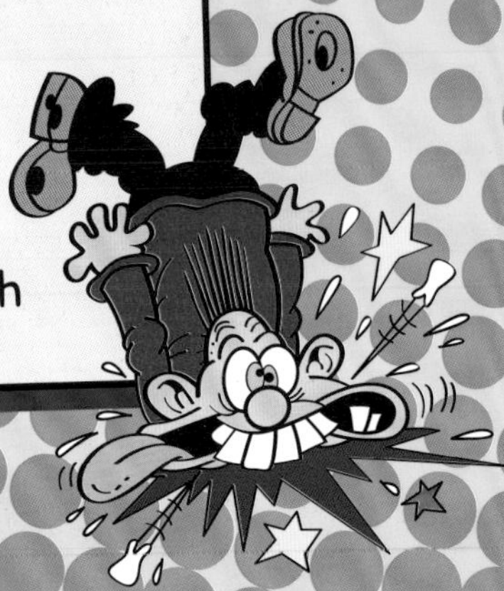

p12 – Beanotown Park

- ☐ A yeti
- ☐ A missing drone
- ☐ A tyre swing
- ☐ Billy Whizz
- ☐ A mole
- ☐ JJ

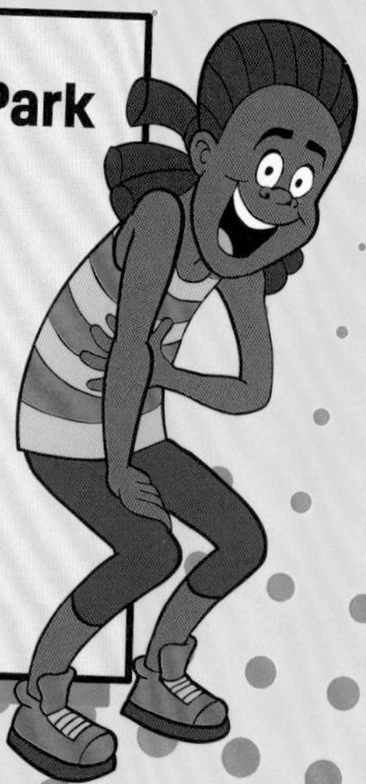

p14 – Duck Island

- ☐ A triceratops
- ☐ A lost frisbee
- ☐ A thirsty man-eating plant
- ☐ Two fighter pilots
- ☐ A duck
- ☐ A T. rex

p16 – Beanotown High Street

- ☐ A whoopee cushion
- ☐ A postbox
- ☐ A squelchy with a hat
- ☐ Roger the Dodger
- ☐ A statue wearing a traffic cone
- ☐ A flowery shopping bag

p18 – Town Hall

- ☐ Future Dennis
- ☐ A lie detector
- ☐ Foo Foo the poodle
- ☐ The mayor's missing chain
- ☐ An ice lolly
- ☐ A red skateboard

p20 - Beanotown Library

- ☐ A stolen love story
- ☐ Pie Face
- ☐ A bookworm
- ☐ Minnie's lost library card
- ☐ Les Pretend
- ☐ A stack of Beano annuals

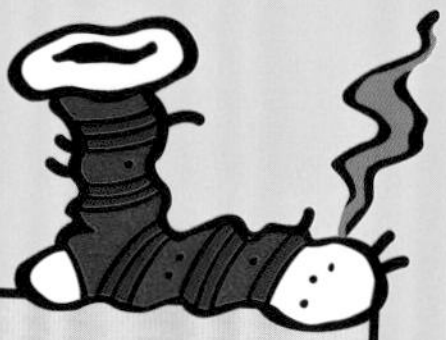

p22 - Beanotown Museum

- ☐ An antique sock
- ☐ Thor's toothpick
- ☐ Toots
- ☐ A bag of stolen gold
- ☐ A sleeping security guard
- ☐ A mummy

p24 - Horrible Hall

- ☐ The Headless Headmaster
- ☐ Betty and Yeti in costume
- ☐ A cyclops
- ☐ A portrait of Walter's grandfather
- ☐ A torch
- ☐ A two-headed worm

p26 - Mount Beano

- ☐ A snow Gnasher
- ☐ Rodney the Red Ram
- ☐ A campfire
- ☐ A polka-dot scarf
- ☐ A hot chocolate
- ☐ Tricky Dicky

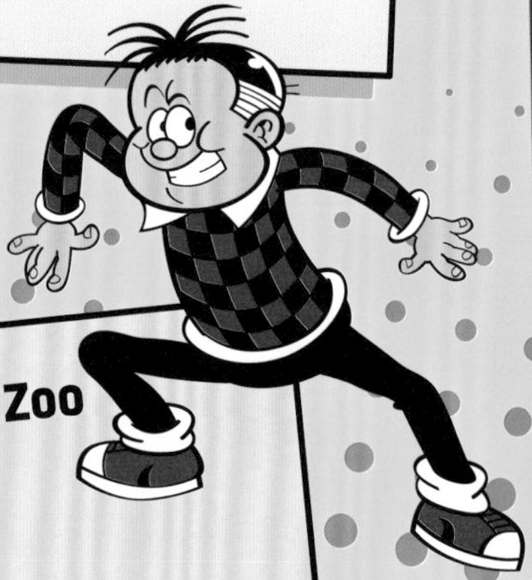

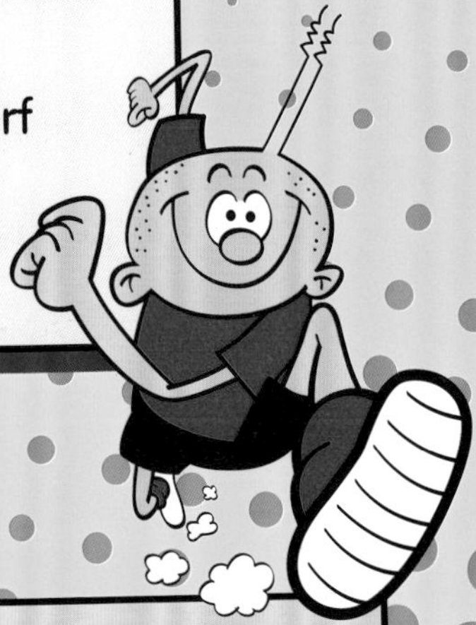

p28 - Beanotown Zoo

- ☐ Big Eggo
- ☐ Pink candyfloss
- ☐ Roger the Dodger
- ☐ An escaping gorilla
- ☐ An unusual zookeeper
- ☐ The zookeeper's missing keys

p30 - Beanotown-on-Sea

- ☐ Pirate's treasure
- ☐ A cat
- ☐ Billy Whizz
- ☐ A snorkeller
- ☐ A red-and-black striped towel
- ☐ A lost penguin

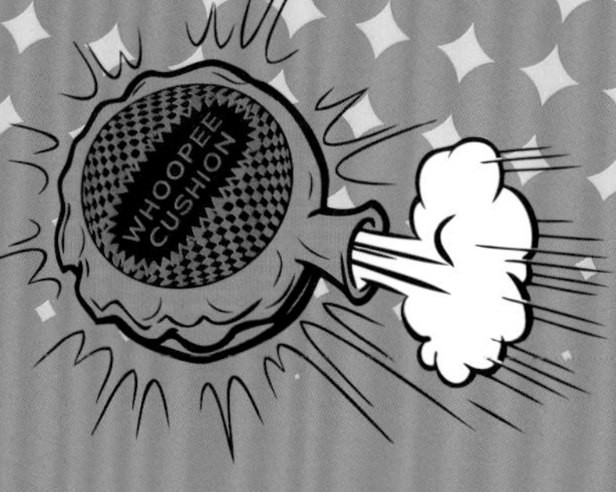
WHOOPEE CUSHION

p32 - Beanotown Police Station

- ☐ A crowbar
- ☐ Dr Gloom
- ☐ A box of doughnuts
- ☐ An escape route
- ☐ A confiscated catapult
- ☐ Stolen sausages

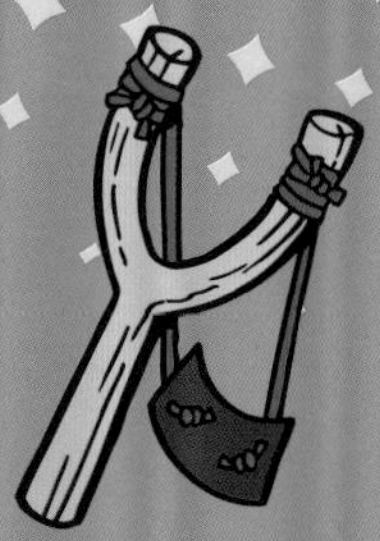

ANSWERS

Dennis, Gnasher, Minnie, Gnipper, Walter and Bea are circled in yellow, and other characters and objects are circled in red.

Did you find them all?

51 Gasworks Road

Bash Street School

Beanotown Tunnels

36

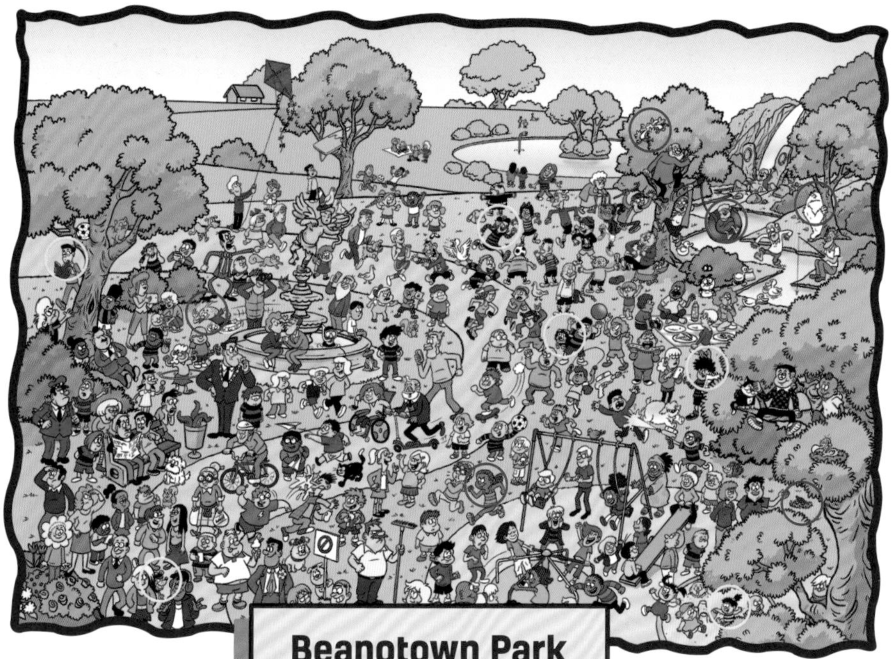

Beanotown Park

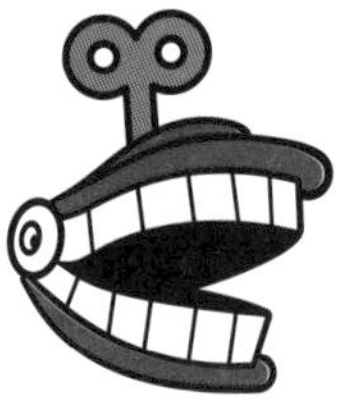

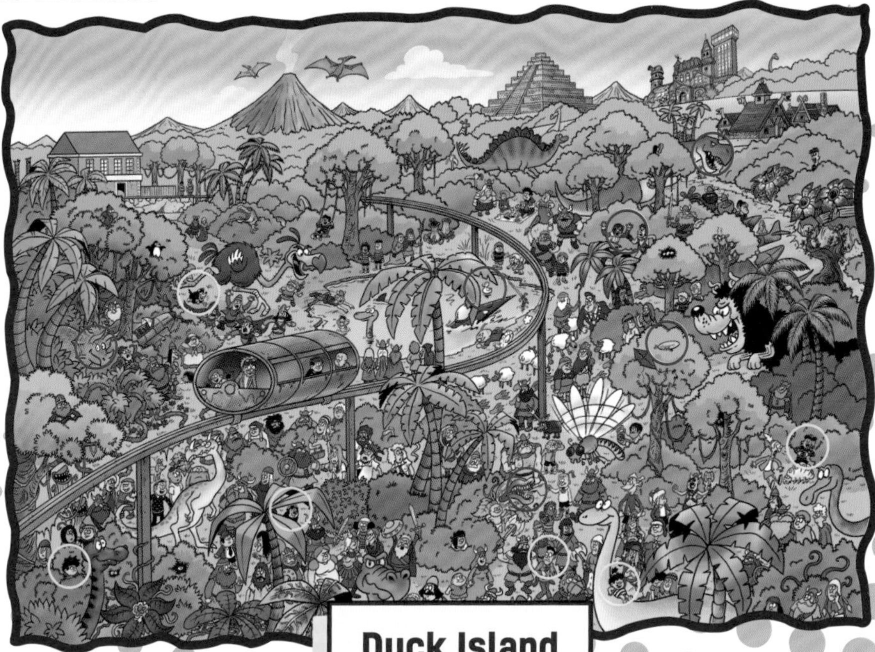

Duck Island

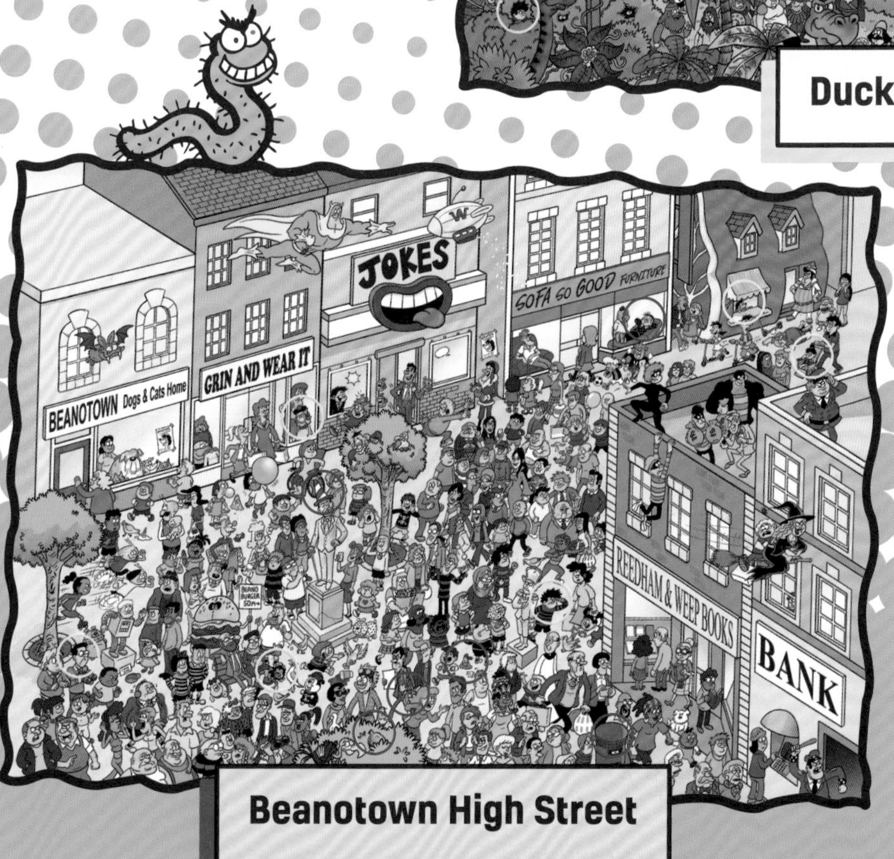

JOKES
SOFA SO GOOD FURNITURE
BEANOTOWN Dogs & Cats Home
GRIN AND WEAR IT
REEDHAM & WEEP BOOKS
BANK

Beanotown High Street

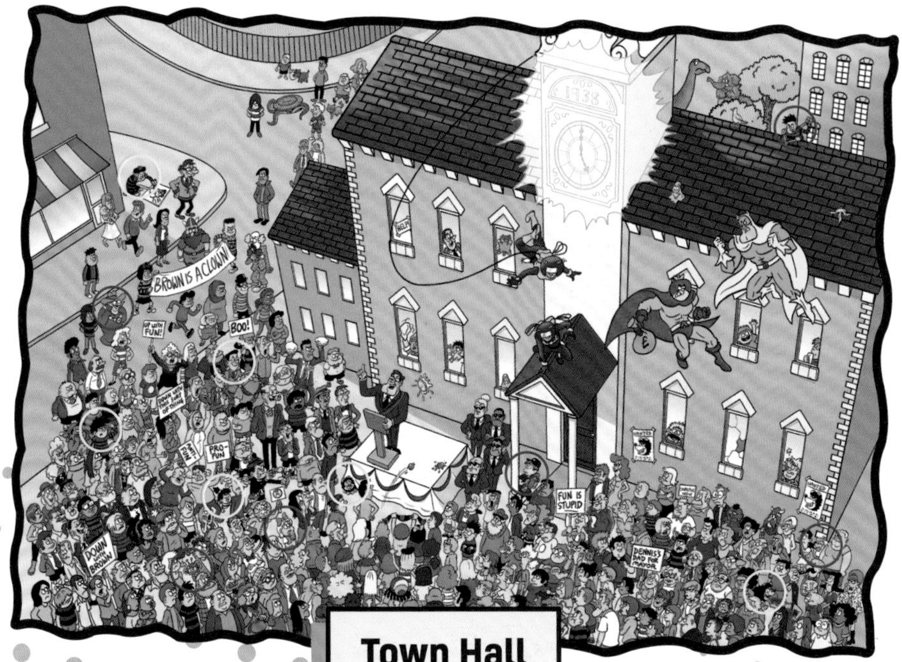
BROWN IS A CLOWN
BOO!
FUN IS STUPID

Town Hall

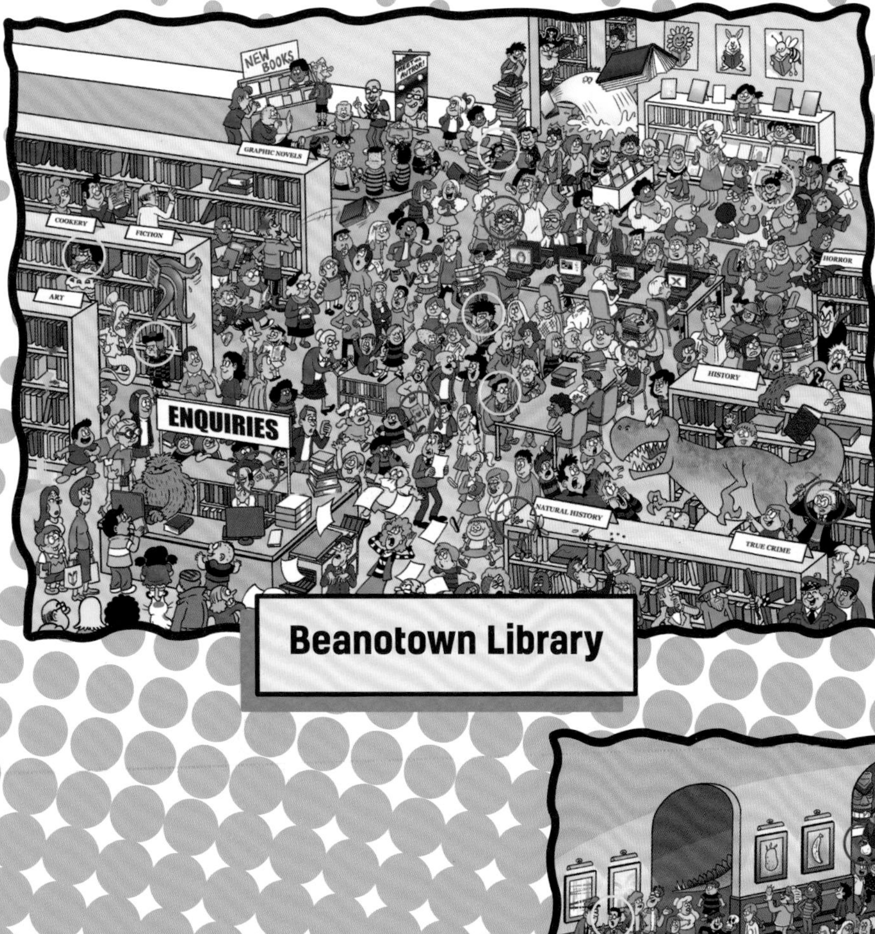
NEW BOOKS
GRAPHIC NOVELS
COOKERY
FICTION
ART
HORROR
HISTORY
ENQUIRIES
NATURAL HISTORY
TRUE CRIME

Beanotown Library

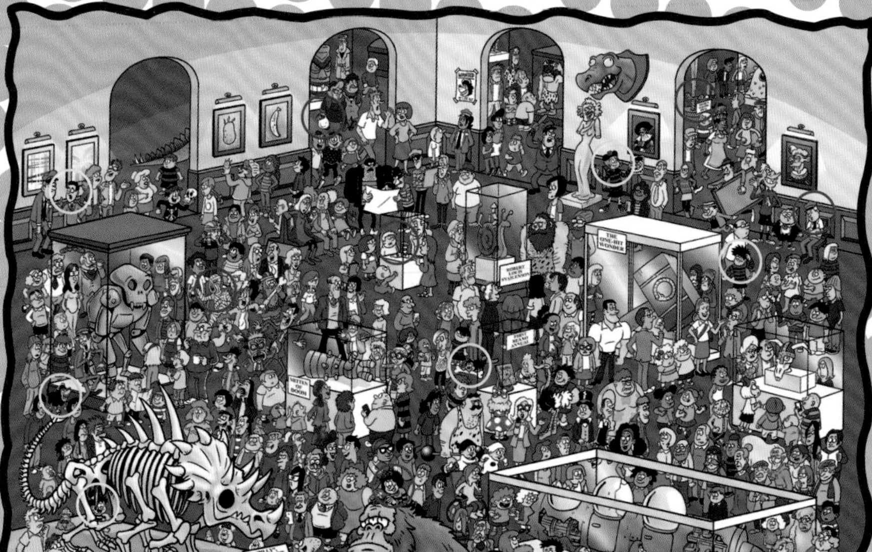

Beanotown Museum

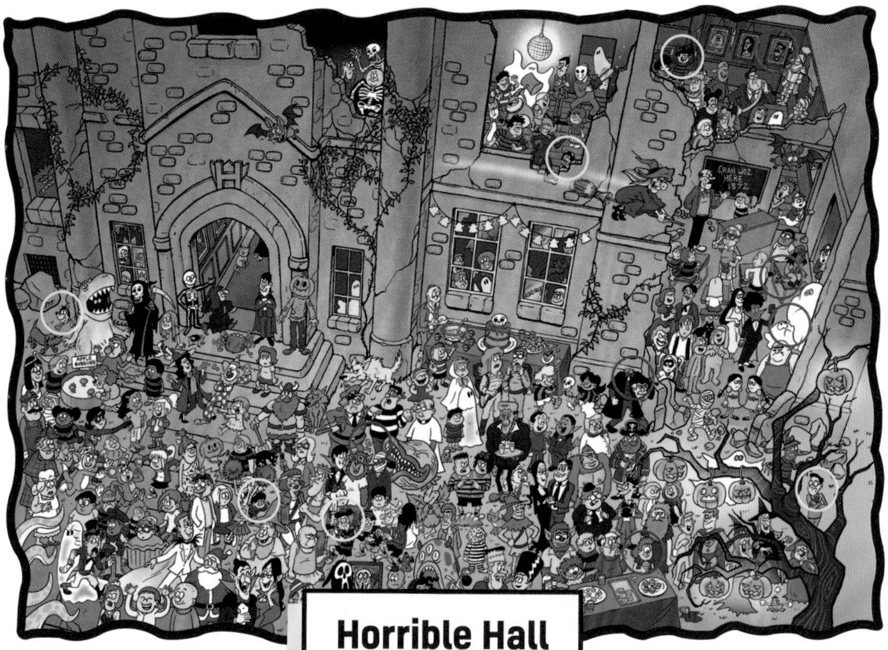

Horrible Hall

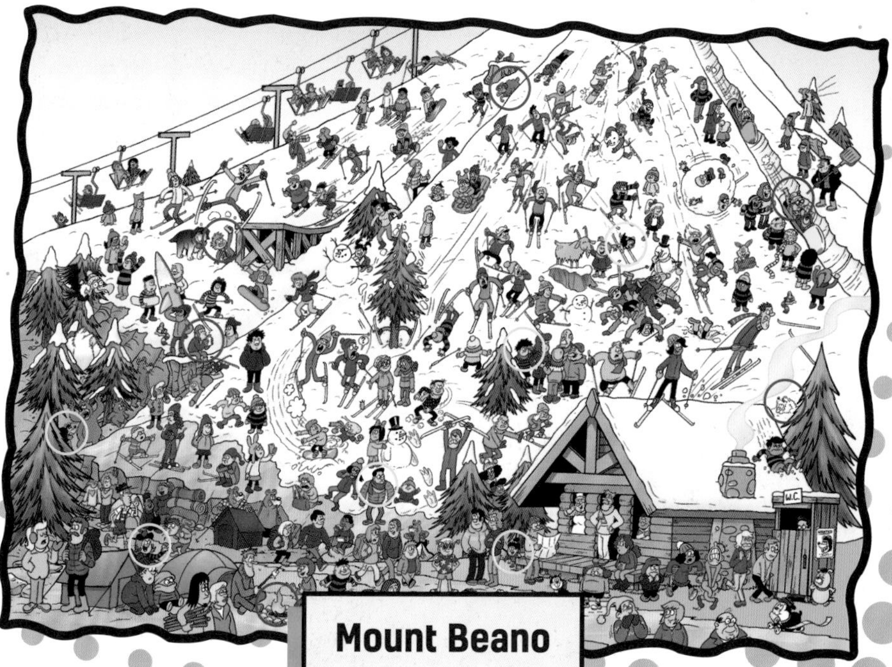
W.C.

Mount Beano

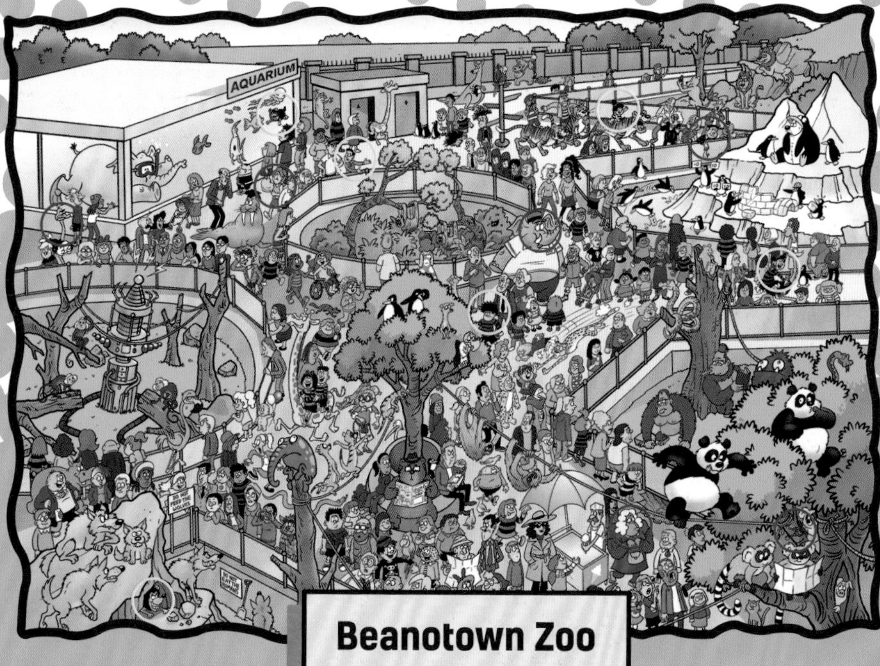
AQUARIUM

Beanotown Zoo

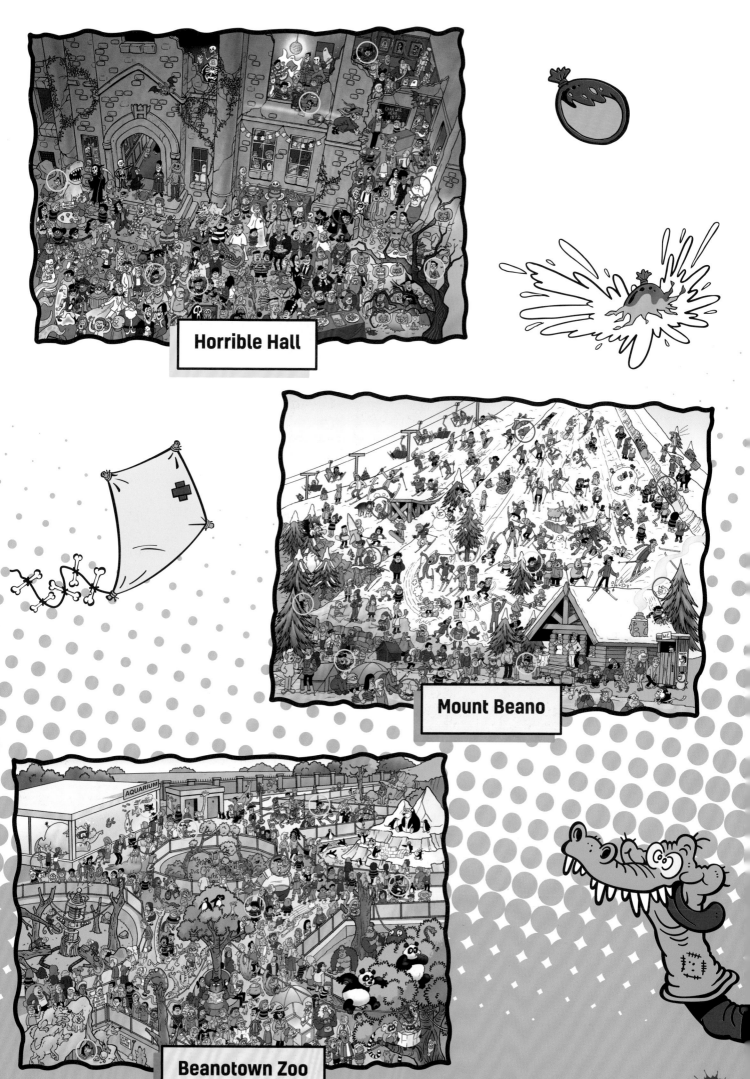

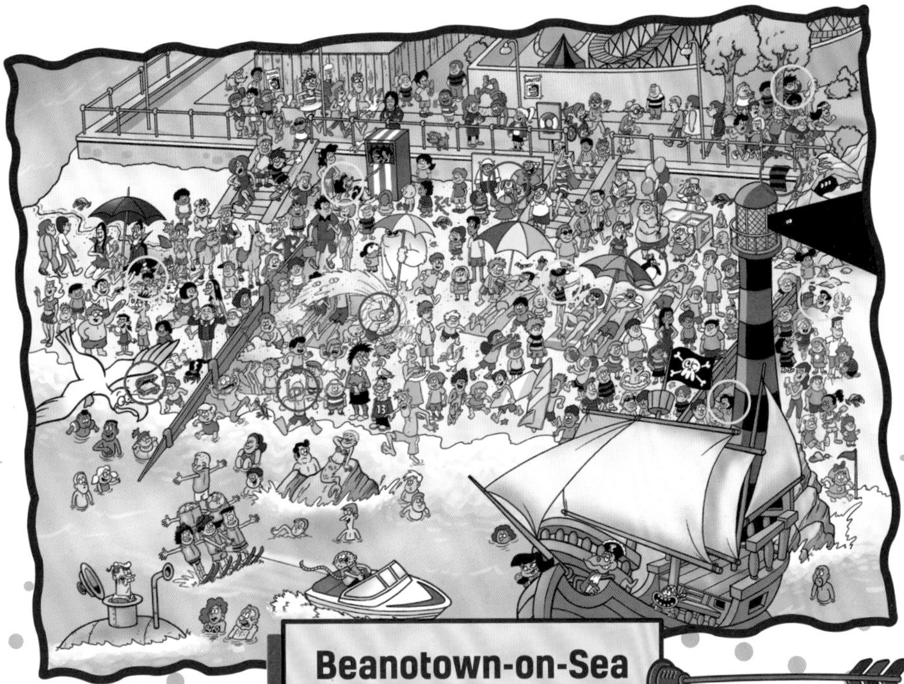

Beanotown-on-Sea

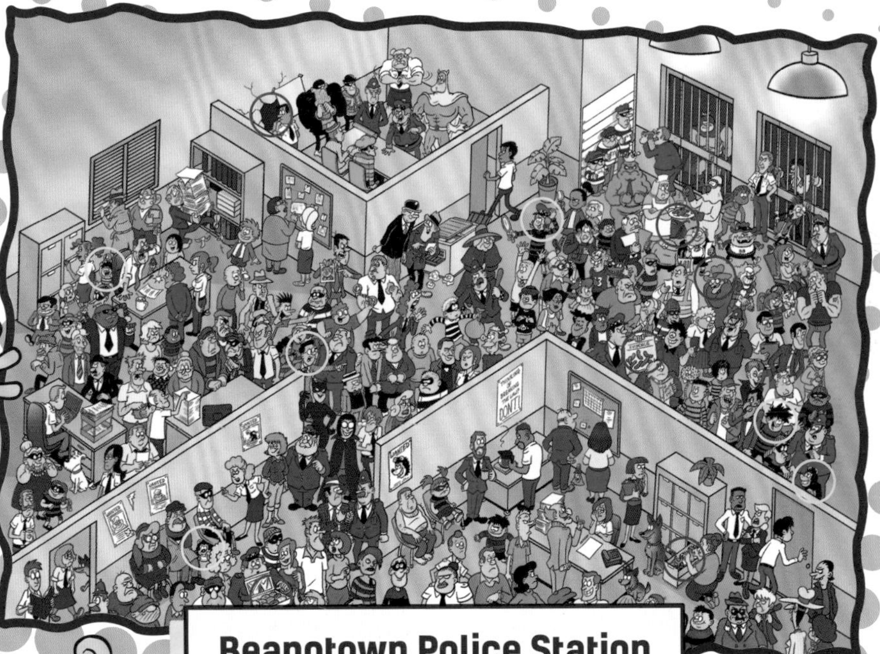

Beanotown Police Station

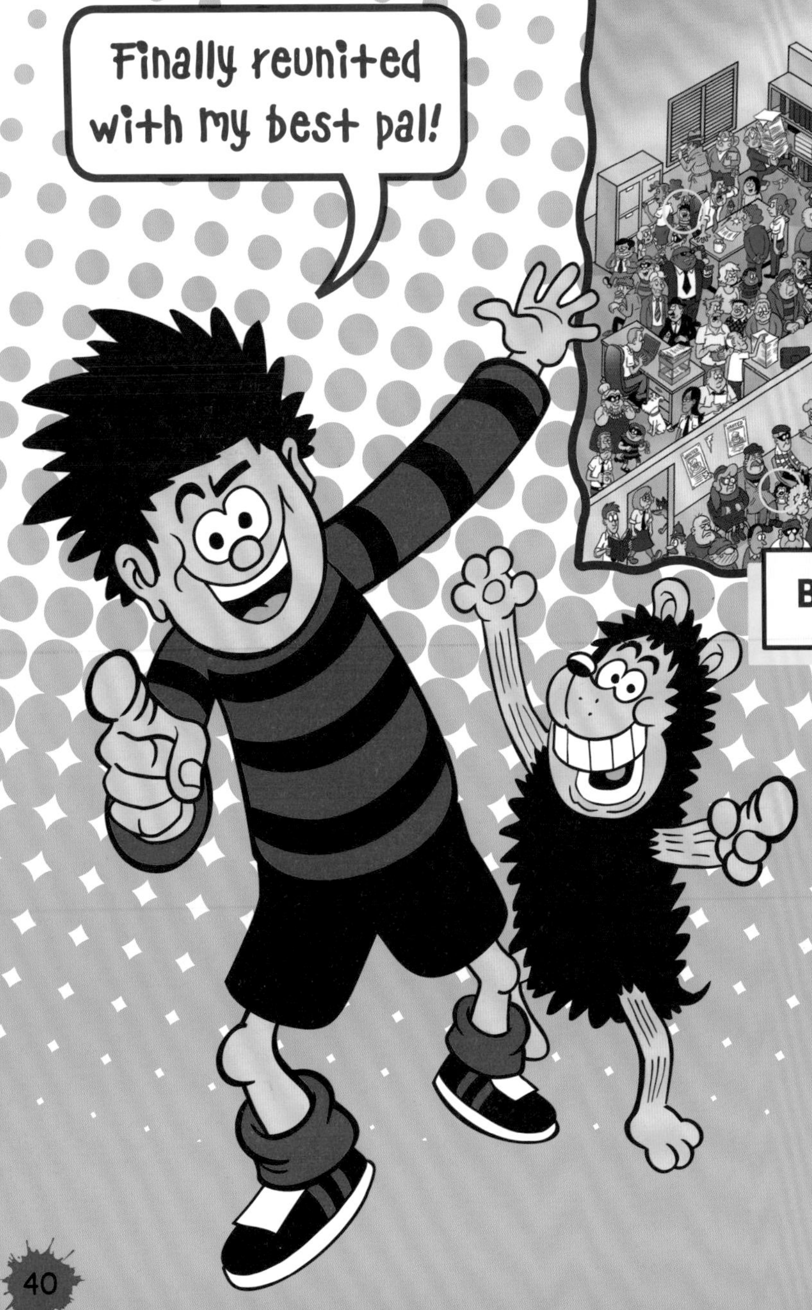
Finally reunited with my best pal!